PYRO
BE

The step-by-step guide to Master the art of Wood burning

By Antony Wood

© Copyright 2021 by Antony Wood

All rights reserved.

This document is geared towards providing exact and reliable information with regards to the topic and issue covered. The publication is sold with the idea that the publisher is not required to render accounting, officially permitted, or otherwise, qualified services. If advice is necessary, legal or professional, a practiced individual in the profession should be ordered.

From a Declaration of Principles which was accepted and approved equally by a Committee of the American Bar Association and a Committee of Publishers and Associations.

In no way is it legal to reproduce, duplicate, or transmit any part of this document in either electronic means or in printed format. Recording of this publication is strictly prohibited and any storage of this document is not allowed unless with written permission from the publisher. All rights reserved.

The information provided herein is stated to be truthful and consistent, in that any liability, in terms of inattention or otherwise, by any usage or abuse of any policies, processes, or directions contained within is the solitary and utter responsibility of the recipient reader. Under no circumstances will any legal responsibility or blame be held against the publisher for any reparation, damages, or monetary loss due to the information herein, either directly or indirectly.

Respective authors own all copyrights not held by the publisher.

The information herein is offered for informational purposes solely, and is universal as so. The presentation of the information is without contract or any type of guarantee assurance.

The trademarks that are used are without any consent, and the publication of the trademark is without permission or backing by the trademark owner. All trademarks and brands within this book are for clarifying purposes only and are the owned by the owners themselves, not affiliated with this document.

TABLE OF CONTENTS

INTRODUCTION 8

CHAPTER 1 11

A Brief History of Pyrography or Wood Burning Art 11

CHAPTER 2 17

Techniques Of Wood-Burning 17

CHAPTER 3 21

The Principles of Woodburning Pyrography 21

CHAPTER 4 25

Important Factors in the Art of Pyrography 25

CHAPTER 5 31

Basic Supplies For Woodburning Art 31

CHAPTER 6 45

Different Types of Wood-Burning Equipment 45

CHAPTER 7 49

Best Woods To Use For Pyrography 49

CHAPTER 8 57

How To Work With Woodgrain In Your Woodburning Pyrography 57

CHAPTER 9 63

How Do You Get Pyrography Started? 63

CHAPTER 10 74
Pyrography Projects For Beginners 74
How To Burn Necks And Chins 77
How To Woodburn Realistic Fur 79
The Art of Drawing Dogs on Wood 84
How to Make The Walking Stick Exclusive 85
CHAPTER 11 88
How to Become An Expert Pyrographer 88
CHAPTER 12 93
Ideas For A First Move To Learn Pyrography 93
CHAPTER 13 98
Shapes To Assist You In Creating Your Designs 98
CHAPTER 14 101
How To Find Inspirational Ideas For Pyrography Projects 101
CHAPTER 15 107
Getting The Most Out Of A Day At An Arts And Crafts Show 107
CHAPTER 16 111
Small Pyrography Business Start-Up Suggestions ... 111
CHAPTER 17 117

Take Advantage Of Every Chance To Promote Your Pyrography Business.. 117

CHAPTER 18 123

Frequently Asked Questions 123

CHAPTER 19 128

Tips To Make A Fortune Out Of Your Pyrography Art Passion.. 128

CONCLUSION 136

INTRODUCTION

Like many others, you might have recently developed an interest in woodcrafts. Woodworkers engage in a variety of tasks, including furniture and toy making. While rewarding, most woodshops necessitate a lot of space and a significant investment in equipment.

Wood burning or Pyrography is a woodcraft hobby with little room and only a small investment in materials. While having a dedicated area to work and store tools is useful, this room does not need to be big. In fact, for most projects, a tiny, sturdy table will suffice.

The art of wood-burning is simple to master! A wood-burning pen with patterns, interchangeable points, sandpaper, graphite paper and wood sealer is everything you'll need to get started. The majority of the other things you'll need are typical household items.

The wood-burning pens from Walnut Hollow Farm are the best choice. There are two basic pens: twenty-six and twenty-one watts. The 26 watt is suitable for all types of wood, most importantly the harder ones. The twenty-one watt is an outstanding first pen. It works best on softer trees.

Depending on the point used, different burning methods are used. Before moving on to intermediate and advanced designs, begin with a basic pattern and learn how to use the many different points.

Basswood is the best wood to start with because it burns quickly. Basswood comes in a range of shapes and sizes, including ovals, rounds, planks and barrel staves. Wooden boxes in some types may also be used as projects. For better results, the wood surface to be burned must be very smooth. With a very fine grade of sandpaper, sand the wood to the finest finish possible.

Graphite or white transfer paper is used to transfer the pattern to the wood surface. On light wood, use graphite paper and on dark wood, use white transfer paper. The template and transfer paper are taped to the wood with masking tape and the design is traced on the wood with a fine point ball-point pen.

There are various burning techniques and woodburning tips to use with the pen to achieve various results. Oil-colored pencils and oil paint wash can also be used to color the burnings. The mixture of wood grain, woodburning and oil paints results in some breathtakingly beautiful artwork.

The possibilities for wood-burning art projects are virtually endless, ranging from jewelry boxes, ring boxes, cutlery boxes, clocks, chairs, and burn designs. You can burn woodcarvings to give your woodcraft projects a one-of-a-kind touch. Woodburning or Pyrography is also a good choice for wall hangings and picture frames.

With this art, you can take your wood art to the next level! Are you ready to explore the basics of Pyrography as a beginner?

Let's get started

CHAPTER 1

A Brief History of Pyrography or Wood Burning Art

Pyrography is one of the oldest art styles, with examples ranging from early cave grafts to ancient burnt decorations on everyday household items. In marquetry, a technique is known as "sand burning" creates shadow effects on the edges of inlaid wood.

Hot coals were used to create "Poker Art," as it was once known. During the Victorian era, pyrography was at its peak. Back then, they used butane torches with open flames. While other companies manufactured butane burner systems, the company that popularized the art form was dubbed "Flemish art."

Butane torches were replaced by electrically operated versions starting in 1916. Although some artists still prefer the old ways, the majority of us prefer the safer alternative. The popularity of pyrographic art has resurfaced.

Museum and historical society curators are now attempting to reclaim antique artifacts from private collections. Many fine pyrographers around the world are introducing this form of art to a new audience. The march of time continues.

Pyrography is a type of art that people from all over the world practice. Combining designs into wood surfaces necessitates the use of heated metal tools. Cups, pots, chests and furniture are examples of pyrographically carved objects. Light-colored woods such as birch, beech, sycamore and basswood and pine and oak were commonly used in this craft.

Pyrography is a concept that has only recently been coined to describe this form of work of art. It is derived from Greek and means "writing with fire." Other terms for the process include woodburning and pokerwork. Pyrography was a term used in the early 1900s. Pyrography has been a part of world cultures' art practices for thousands of years and is still used today.

According to evidence from China, Egypt, Rome, and Peru, pyrography has existed in some form since ancient times. Pyrography was regarded as a "stick of a fire needle" in China during the Han Dynasty. To burn wood designs, early craftsmen used heated metal rods of various sizes.

The early pyrographic artworks of Peru's Nazca and Moche cultures are well-known. One of the earliest representations of the South American pyrograph was a Nazca mate cup from about 700 AD. The nectar beverages are graved in this small wooden cup.

Pyrography artists used newly created portable wood pots as a source of heat in the Middle Ages. These kitchen burners had tiny holes in their lids that allowed pokers to pass through.

The pokers remained in the holes until they were warm enough to use, then they were heated over the stove charcoals. Artists sometimes carried many pokers with them to keep working as other pokers heated up.

While poker was chosen, other sharp metal objects such as needles and knives were used. Because of the craft's style, it's obvious that medieval blacksmiths practiced pyrography. Pyrography and blacksmithing also used hot springs and many blacksmiths used the heat from their forges to manufacture metal and wood.

The twentieth-century pyrography

At the turn of the century, a Melbourne architect called Alfred Smart discovered a more modern and accurate pyrography method. He discovered that benzene fumes could be pumped using a heated hollow pencil.

This allowed the pyrographic tools to stay hot during the process. The platinum pencil came with a benzene bottle and a rubber ball squeezed into the pencil to stir the fumes.

This new method allowed artists to create tints and shades in wood that were previously impossible to achieve. Smart's discovery was bolstered by the fact that he was finally electrified.

Until the late nineteenth century, pyrography was dominated by men. The invention of domestic pyrographic machines and kits popularized the craft, making it accessible to women who needed to decorate their homes with handicrafts. Pyrography kits were promoted as a good fit for young women in various publications, including catalogs and female magazines.

Bassets are inexpensive and allow women to create beautiful pieces in their own homes to decorate or sell to others. Small projects, such as frames and handkerchief boxes, are normally completed by women but large pieces of furniture, such as armoires and chairs, may also be burned.

Pyrography has grown to meet the needs and aspirations of the times since its ancient beginnings. Artists used wood burning to add charm and beauty to everyday items in the early years, medieval times, and the century's turn on almost every continent. Pyrography is and will continue to be significant in the arts of cultures all over the world.

A woodburning tool is always needed, regardless of what you're burning. It also shouldn't be too expensive; you can burn just as well with a cheap wood burning tool as you can with a professional burning unit.

CHAPTER 2

Techniques Of Wood-Burning

Pyrography art entails decorating wood with burn marks produced by a hot object such as a metal style. The Greek words "pyro" and "graphics" are translated as "writing with fire." The ancient art of pyrography is said to have originated in caves but it may date back to the Han Dynasty (206 BC-220 AD) when it was known as a fire needle stick.

Pyrography, also known as wood burning produces many exquisitely beautiful and insightful works of art. It's a great way for talented designers to play with new materials and develop stunning decorative designs.

Various plumbing and equipment tips allow you to create various brushstrokes for various effects, while different pressure levels allow you to achieve different color tones.

Before getting started with pyrography, you'll need the following items:

A pyrography dye.

A strong softwood piece

A good polishing agent for sandpaper

A holder for the stylus

You should be able to get everything you need with a decent pyrography starter kit. This comes with a pyrograph, stylus, stand and five screw tips as part of the wood-burning tool kit. The box is also an excellent place to put your skills to the test.

In pyrography, where wildlife, swirling patterns, animals and geometric prints are popular, monochromatic images and designs are better suited.

Preparing the Wood

You must use beautiful softwood such as oak, ash or maple. It is easier to burn and lighter in color, allowing for better contrast in your work. I must sand down the wood with 320-grit sandpaper and move into the grain.

Clean the surface with a damp cloth later to ensure it is dust-free and clean. The smooth surface makes it easier to transfer your idea and produce a clearer finished product.

You should feel secure enough to let go of your concept. If not, you can transfer your template's pattern to the wood. A good way to do so is with graphite or carbon paper. Simply print the template you want, lay the carbon paper on top of the wood and draw the contours. You can also use plain tracing paper.

It's a good idea to get ideas for your projects from social media sites like Instagram or Pinterest. Instagram's content has been imported. You can find the same material in a different format on their website or learn more about them.

You can experiment with a variety of nibs. Before turning on your pen, put the nib you want to use in the holder. Before attempting the final design, it is a good idea to try a sample wood.

Wood-burning methods

1. Use soft strokes and don't overwork your pyrography technique. Create a series of color layers ranging from light to dark. Light areas can be easily darkened but not the other way around. Sandpaper may also be used to correct an error but it will not work if the area is too dark.

2. When the wood is burnt, go with the grain, so place the pen so that the grain is facing you when you pull the pen to you. Going against the grain will make resistance more difficult to achieve.

3. It's a good idea to start with the outline of your picture and then fill in the details.

4. Take the time to clean up your tips, as carbon buildup will minimize the ink's effectiveness. You can use aluminum oxide on your ink if the weather is cool.

CHAPTER 3

The Principles of Woodburning Pyrography

Pyrography, also known as woodburning, is a beautiful and easy-to-do alternative to traditional drawing and painting. Fortunately, it's also fairly simple to master once you realize that pyrography is a physical rather than a mechanical process that can't be approached in the same way that drawing or painting can.

Drawing and painting are primarily mechanical, requiring ink, graphite or paint, whereas pyrography is primarily physical. When I say physical, I'm referring to the fact that the marks are created by heat. Heat causes the surface to change physically, resulting in your marks.

In other words, instead of laying in color, you're changing the surface's physical properties. Instead proper pen care. The most common mistake is not cleaning the tips. Carbon will build up on the pen as you burn it, affecting the heat. The pen tip will be insulated, directing heat up toward the handle and making it uncomfortable to burn.

Regularly clean your pen to keep it in good condition. While the pen is still hot, use a metal tea strainer to scrape away any carbon buildup gently. Use a leather strop or fine sanding block to clean the tips after the pen has cooled. This will keep your pens in good working order and extend their life. It will also assist you in drawing neat lines with the least amount of effort.

These three principles will assist you in mastering pyrography more quickly and reducing your learning curve.

CHAPTER 4

Important Factors in the Art of Pyrography

When using the medium of pyrography, there are a variety of important factors to remember. First and foremost, it's important to understand what this word means and what art form it represents. When a word is split, it comes from Greek. "Pyro" is the first element, which means "fire." The second aspect, "graphy," refers to the act of writing.

While this means "fire writing," we'll just call it wood burning. We're going to start with the history of this amazing art form. I intend to write a few papers about pyrography or wood-burning, including various instruments, how to use them, and different techniques.

Pyrography has been known to have been used by Egyptians and African tribes since ancient times. Wood-burning, also known as "fire needle embroidery" in China, was very common during the Han Dynasty. Pyrographic machines were built during the Victorian period (circa 1890) and are credited with popularizing wood burning.

Before being renamed pyrography, this art form was known as "poker burning." Wood stoves and drills were used in pre-Victorian England to poke holes in the fabric or wood they were working on. The Vulcan Wood Etching Machine made it easier, more fun and added a new comfort level to the medium, which drew many Victorian women.

The techniques used for wood burning are very different from the cultures mentioned since our instruments have been adapted and updated with modern technologies. I strongly advise you to Google the word "pyrography" to see for yourself the completely stunning creations created by artisans all over the world using a variety of tools and locations.

You can burn wood and paper, gourds, cloth and stuff, bark, tagua, leather, seeds, nuts, horns, teeth and antlers (with caution). And cork can be combustible. As you can see, the only limit to this medium is your imagination. You can either build your archetype or choose from a library of pre-made symbols, shapes and patterns. If you don't want to make your crafts, there are websites where you can purchase these exclusive craft types.

Since the invention of pyrography, derived from pure Greek (fire) and graphics (writing), cavemen undoubtedly grated their caves walls with burning sticks, despite the lack of hard evidence. Though it was (and still is) mainly done on wood with heated ink, it was also done on cloth, clay and even gourds.

Different instruments and musical instruments have been designed and branded throughout history. Kitchenware and folk guitars were labeled with artwork to express their personalities and set them apart from the competition.

Soldering plums were developed at the turn of the twentieth century, from which today's wood-burning tools evolved. This is a project that both men and children will appreciate (under adult supervision, of course). Fortunately, the initial costs are minimal and studying is a simple pastime. Woodburning may be a source of DIY gifts for the family for years to come. There are many different kinds of techniques in the art of pyrography. I'll try to break it down for you to find out what's right for you.

There are two kinds of "burners" on the market. Please read them carefully to ensure that you are acquainted with them.

Variable temperature data burners with a craft style solid tip

Strong tips in the craft style are ideal for basic crafts that do not require detailed work. A good example of this style of work is signed. However, if the tips are of low quality, they can easily bend and break. Their thinness can measure the consistency of these tips. Make some comparisons (preferably in person) so you can see the differences for yourself.

Visit the shops to see what's available and get a sense of what you're looking for. Then you can buy it there or order it online. It's always a good idea to see what you're doing before you buy it. This will reduce the number of returns if you are disappointed with a purchase.

The craft-style solid tip burners have the disadvantage of being big and heavy, which causes your hand to fatigue quickly. They can also take up to ten minutes to heat or cool. The tips must be screwed in with extreme caution and only after they have cooled.

Otherwise, your threading would be damaged. Some of these burners have a good heat shield to keep your hand secure. They're also better than variable temperature burners at burning big, dark areas quickly.

Now it's time to talk about variable-temperature burners.

These have many settings for heating your tip, as the name implies. This is useful for fine detail work where finer lines and less heat are desired. You'll get a more even heat flow with higher-quality tips.

Fixed-tip and interchangeable-tip pens are available from different companies.

These pens or burners do not burn as quickly as craft burners, so patience and a steady hand are needed but keep in mind that the devil is in the details.

It's safer to burn these in layers and at a lower temperature. It's a lot easier to add more burn than to remove it (though it is possible!). Burning in layers will give you a more professional appearance.

CHAPTER 5

Basic Supplies For Woodburning Art

Some important tools or supplies must accompany a beginner and expert pyrographer in his artwork. The basic supplies are listed below:

A woodburning pen

There are a variable heat control and a case for different tips, which I like. It costs twice as much but it's still just $20. It's as cheap and low-end as it gets but I've been doing fine for more than six months. If you're working in pyrography, you can get styluses for hundreds of dollars.

A woodburning pen is a very straightforward tool. It's a pen with a metal end that transfers heat to a tip that can be removed. Everything but the cheapest tools has variable temperature settings.

Each kit includes 4-7 tips for various burning techniques, such as rounded lines, straight lines shading and so on. You'll also have a metal safety stand for the pen, which will keep it from sitting on a table or workbench.

The first step in every project should be to familiarize yourself with the process. Get a piece of wood, plug it into the wood-burning tool and let it heat up for about 5 minutes before trying your hand at "drawing" on the wood with various tips, just like a crayon.

It's as easy as that. (Before changing tips, let your instrument cool for 5 minutes; it will need to be heated up again for a few minutes.) You'll show that you're jerky if you're jerky. If you leave too soon, the wood will not burn as efficiently as you would like. The race progresses slowly and steadily, just like the tortoise.

The circular tip is the one on the left. It may be the one I use the most. The shading tip is on the right. Since the floor is flat, you can burn a greater surface area at the same time. The rounded tip on the left is the one I use the most and is very versatile. The shading tip is on the right; note the flat floor, which allows you to simultaneously burn a larger surface area.

After you've purchased a burning machine and gathered your basic equipment, it's time to choose some burning materials. Though wood is the most popular medium for pyrography, it is not the only one.

Paper, leather, gourds, bark, nuts and ivory are among the items that can be pyrographed. They each have their own set of challenges and benefits. The material is wood. Many trees may be burned but some are better suited to pyrography than others.

The burnt picture and the board are best contrasted with light-colored wood. Dark wood may also be used but the burned image may blend into the background, particularly after being burned. When it comes to burning a blank canvas, most people prefer wood with the smallest possible grain.

Working with heavily seeded wood is more challenging but the results can be spectacular if the grain is incorporated into the design. The hardest wood can be burned with a powerful pyrographic machine; nevertheless, soft and evenly textured wood burns well and leaves a clear impression in the wood if you want to texture a large amount of wood.

Consider using high-quality furnishings or chairs to frame and suspend your work. Signs, functional pieces and wall suspensions can all benefit from strong wood planks. Wood that hasn't lost its bark edge creates a natural and productive self-framed surface to burn.

Untreated frames, kitchen utensils, boxes, pots and other functional parts are made of wood blanks. The majority of these woods can be used in crafts, woodcarving and wood shops in the United States and Canada.

Pyrography is also used to decorate furniture. With a little time and creativity, a cheap pine coffee table can be transformed into a family heirloom. A single touch may be applied to a home's wooden components, such as a kitchen cabinet. It is important to remember that wood that has already been processed or sealed is not burned.

Burning leather is a pleasurable experience. There is no way to compromise or fight wood grain. The heated nib is cooler than wood and sinks into the floor, allowing you to draw quickly and smoothly. Leather is also very adaptable.

It can be shown alone in a frame or applied to realistic items like dog collars, straps and bags. There are a few disadvantages to using leather. Leather burning stank slightly compared to wood burning, and it can quickly gum up and dirty your nibs. You'll also need to get your tip.

If you don't, your nib will stick to the surface and bounce around, sometimes leaving dirt behind. Leather is both cheaper and more difficult to come by than wood. I drive a long distance to choose

Clean, Smooth, good-quality hand leather

The easiest way to find a supplier is to look in the phone book or on the Internet for leather dealers.

Cowhides are the most popular and easiest to come by but many others, such as buckskin orange peel and kangaroo, can be used as long as they're vegetable-tanned and haven't been handled with chromium wax or oil.

Many soft pieces of leather are bleached or chromium-tanned and the fumes from burning them can be hazardous to your health. If you have any questions, please inquire. Unless you're going for a three-dimensional effect, leather thickness isn't all that important.

Alternatively, heavily prick when smoking. All of your regular nibs, including a shader, askew and writing nibs, make surface burning easy. Cover your leather from dirt and moisture with leather or leather lacquer if your finished product is handled regularly. If the piece is flat and rigid, varnish spray may be used.

A piece of paper

Paper holds up well in a fire. Paper pyrography is not only feasible but also aesthetically pleasing. It requires a more cautious and gentle approach than other pyrographic forms. The beauty of paper burning is that you never have to spend time searching for the perfect piece of wood – it's all waiting for you at the art store.

It's cheap, plentiful and simple to structure and present. Acid-free rag paper can be used both hot and cold-pressed. The texture of the cold-pressed paper is rough, while the texture of the hot-pressed paper is smooth. Because of its large surface area, smooth paper is often the best choice for beginners.

However, don't dismiss the rough paper's ability to create romantic and rustic effects or moods. The paper's thickness is determined by the impact you want to achieve and your level of expertise. You can burn on thin paper but you risk punching through it and you'll be limited in how noisy and textured you can be.

You can also use colorless illustration cardboard to strongly texture and graze the paper. You can generate some interesting effects by burning colored paper and cartons. For your safety, keep in mind what chemicals or dyes were used to color the paper.

Gourds

The combination of pyrography and gourds lends itself to natural and realistic designs, but abstract shapes and stylized subjects are common and have a great impact compared to other types of wood; gourds burn dirty, so you'll have to clean your nib as you work.

Since gourds are more difficult to burn than flatwork due to their spherical shapes, you'll need to find a comfortable way to hold your work. Both regular nibs work well in gourds, but the gourd's surface is slightly coated and slicker to burn than soft flat wood.

Since this might trigger a weird skid, I prefer to burn my lines with a sharp skew. This knife-like nib tends to catch and fit into the surface, preventing injuries and fostering a crisp, clean line.

The texture seems to work particularly well on gourds because the light hits various angles, so don't be afraid to experiment with patterns. You can also use a hot nib from your gourd shell to physically chop whole bits, giving your work a whole new dimension.

Color can be used in combination with burning if needed. Acrylic paints are my preferred medium but many other pigments, such as leather dyes and pencils, can achieve similar results. I recommend using a spray varnish to cover and protect your work fully.

Tagua

Tagua is also known as "palm ivory" or "vegetable ivory." The dried nut of the ivory palm grows in the Amazon rainforest. (It's worth noting that sustainable tagua logging both prevents and encourages forest destruction.) Tagua is also difficult to come by due to its unique existence.

They can be found in many woodcarving supplies and specialty shops. Because of the unpredictable color and the fact that most nuts have a hole in the center, I prefer to buy individual slices from the vendors.

I enjoy burning on tagua but it's one of the most challenging materials I've ever worked with. Because of its difficulty, sanding by hand takes a long time, so I prefer to use a slow-speed inverted belt sander.

Due to its high oil content, Tagua does not burn as much as a cook and produces a tar-like substance. This strange effect can make some subjects, such as fur, extremely lifelike, particularly if the tagua is burned with a sharp skew.

Nonetheless, I recommend basic subjects for beginners, such as flora or a butterfly; more advanced projects need a lot of practice. Cleaning the nib regularly is sufficient to ensure a smooth, clean burn. I just use the finest nibs and I use a very fine skew for most of the work.

Since a Tagua is burning bleeds on water contact, it's important to spray the finished work many times with a spirit-based acrylic to completely film the pyrograph. It also covers handling, so adequate coverage is needed to protect your work.

Many types of trees produce paperbark, which can be used for pyrography. The barks I tested are needed for both the Australian paperbark and the North American paper birch. Lines had difficulty keeping their edge or coloring because the surface was so soft and spongy.

This created a slightly soft, romantic effect but it was difficult to work with for very detailed work. This is an interesting burn, but I recommend it for high contrast jobs or simple subjects unless you have a hand. The use of silhouettes in this medium gives it a very strong appearance.

Ivory and Bone

Purchasing, selling or exchanging African elephant ivory is illegal unless the stock is pre-embargo. In general, only old piano keys and some old tusk can be used for pyrographic projects.

Ivory from fossilized mastodons can be bought and sold freely but check with your local customs office to see any import/export restrictions. Please keep in mind that purchasing, selling or trading Indian elephant ivory is illegal in any situation. Bone and ivory are not for the faint of heart.

Both of them need a red-hot nib that can break ivory for long periods, requiring the ivory to be burned in short bursts. By burning with a pointy skew, which I frequently turn over to use the tip itself to fit the surface, I achieved the greatest success.

Like scrimshaw with fire, the picture comprises a series of small cuts and incised dots. My only experience with ivory burning so far has been with piano keys and while I found it sticky, hot and stinky, the result can be delicate and appealing.

Horns, teeth and antlers

Rare burning objects include animal horns, teeth and antlers. I haven't had the opportunity to burn antler or horn but I have seen some beautiful pyrographic examples of both, particularly antlers.

The antler's tip can be cut through a disk and used as a pin or a pendulum.

A light-colored area on the antler's flat surface can also be sanded to create the perfect canvas for pyrographic portraits. Nature scenes are usually acceptable and appropriate for this one-of-a-kind platform.

Cork

Due to its soft and bumpy texture, detailed cork burning is minimal. Simpler designs or silhouettes are best suited to this material. Use natural cork that has not been refined or impregnated with chemicals. To preserve the work, either leave the finished picture or spray or varnish it.

Artist's Conk

The tree fungus Ganoderma applanatum (Tree Fungus) is an unusual pyrography method. (Fungus on Trees) Artist's Conk is a fungal growth that looks like a plate and can be seen at the base of a tree trunk or a dead stump.

The plate's top is rough and brown but the creamy white bottom seems to have been burned. If the cone is kept wet, the underside becomes soft and easily labeled, then picked and dried before use. Use art varnish to cover the finished product.

CHAPTER 6

Different Types of Wood-Burning Equipment

Woodburning, also known as pyrography is a basic but highly effective technique. Rustic wedding settings, detailed Christmas trees, gift boxes and even house signs can all be made with it.

We'll go through the basics of pyrography in this chapter, including what equipment and materials you'll need, what techniques you can use and how to get the most out of your work.

For wood-burning, there are two main types of equipment available. They all have benefits and disadvantages, so it all comes down to what you're looking for and how willing you are to pay. The capabilities and price points, on the other hand, are levels. Anything suitable for your requirements can be found in the middle of the road.

Option 1: The Woodburning Pen's First Stage

These tools cost about £20–50 and are ideal if you're just getting started with the craft and don't want to spend £100+ right away. Typically, you will be given some suggestions to consider. The tip is usually made of a solid metal part in various sizes, shapes and thicknesses. The box pictured above is the one I ordered from Amazon for only £20.

Since the solid tip is solid and can dig into the wood if too much tension is applied, these types can be a little more difficult to use than the more expensive soldering irons.

It's good to work with each of the different tips to apply different levels of pressure and temperature choices once you've mastered the various strokes. All the findings shown in these posts were created with this kit.

Option 2: Soldering with Iron

These options usually cost between £80 and £150, suggesting a much higher initial outlay. When this post is published, the model shown above is available on Amazon for £121.

Soldering irons usually have a pen that is attached to a temperature control box. The other major difference with the first choice is that the soldering iron's end tips are usually made of a finely bent wire in various ways rather than a solid metal tip.

You remember the instrument you used in those games, which tests your hand's steadiness as you try to move around a shaped wire without touching it.

For larger crafts or those that need extreme precision, soldering iron is usually the best alternative. It has more strength, more precise strokes and is quicker and easier to use in general.

Of course, the cost is a huge drawback. If you're new to wood burning and aren't sure if it's your thing or if you just use your tool a few times for things like wedding place settings, the cheaper option above could be more appealing.

Whatever option you choose, it's worth spending a few moments looking at the various end sections, temperature settings and different outcomes with various pressure or stroke numbers. I made a test board out of three old pine floorboards that I glued together to do this. It's a great place to relax when working on a real project.

CHAPTER 7

Best Woods To Use For Pyrography

Pyrography is a trend that is steadily gaining popularity by transforming everyday materials into something extraordinary. If you haven't heard of pyrography, it's a form of art that dates back to the 17th century and involves accurate designs, freehand drawings and decorations on a wooden surface using a heated stage.

As a result, your art piece is derived from the dark brand marks you've made and with a little flourish and practice; you can master the shades, shadow and produce beautiful portraits and landscapes on your chosen wood.

However, the first burning question is: which wood do you choose?

Checking how well the finished results would ensure you buy the right wood for your latest pyro art project is critical. In this chapter, Woodshop Direct has published four wooden panels that are simple to work with and show your masterpiece in the best light possible.

Maple syrup

This is a more expensive pyrographic choice but it may be the best wood to work with. Maple is a light to medium-colored wood with a fine grain that brings out all the subtle details in your painting, which you've worked on for hours. Because of the wood's extreme toughness, we recommend using a high-quality heating tool or one that can hit high temperatures while working with maple.

Poplar tree

It's similar to maple in that it's much less expensive. Poplar is a common choice for daily pyrography projects. The light color and subtle grain pattern are ideal for working and the burn patterns you create will be exceptional. The only disadvantage of poplar is the risk of sapphire and resin spots or colors spreading over time but this is only a minor thing to consider while buying.

Jelutong

Jelutong is a flexible material that can be used for some art projects, including carving, patterning, whitening and model making but not just pyrography. This wood is perfect for integrating various artistic disciplines on a single piece of wood.

A beech tree

Beech is a decent alternative to maple and possibly poplar if you're looking for a more affordable option. It has an attractive pale color but when heated, the grain pattern can be esthetic and allow for sap drainage.

What kinds of wood should I stay away from?

Avoid any dark, grainy, resinous wood with an uneven or rough surface; working on these qualities would be difficult, if not impossible.

Avoid forests that have been finished or have synthetic materials in their construction because when heated, they can release harmful chemicals that can be hazardous if inhaled. As a result, we recommend that you avoid using reclaimed wood as well.

Here's a list of the best wood for wood burning with pros and cons:

A. Alder - 3/4" x 2" x 12" - 4 Pack

Owing to the lack of resin, the dark hardwood burns easily and smoothly. It is simple to obtain and is a low-cost alternative.

Benefits

Burns quickly

Don't become a sap.

A less expensive alternative

Drawbacks

Small sizes

Dark-colored wood with a grain pattern

B. Basswood Wooden Sheets, Unfinished

Another cheap and readily available wood has the added advantage of reducing grain and emphasizing tip strokes.

Benefits

Timber at a low cost

Scarcity of sap or resin

Light-colored wood

It is ready to use.

Drawbacks

For certain projects, wood are a little too light.

C. Cherries

Because of its irregular dark color, this reddish-brown hardwood is difficult to work with. However, if you can work with a range of colors, you can create many designs with many promises.

Benefits

There is no sapphire or resin in this product.

Can make some unusual patterns and designs

Drawbacks: It's too dim and the color isn't consistent.

D. Maple syrup

This light-colored wood with a fine grain is ideal for wood-burning. However, it is an expensive wood. However, since it contains no resin, many wood-burning artists prefer it.

Benefits

A light-colored wood

Gouge resistance is strong.

Drawbacks

It's not easy to find

Expensive

E. Albus of the Pacific

When working with this wood, it feels very close to balsa and gives you a hybrid feeling. It's softwood with very little Resin and straw. As a consequence, it's a common option among wood burners.

Benefits

A light-colored wood

Scarcity of sap or resin

Alternative that works

It can be twisted and shaped.

Drawbacks

The heat has the power to distort it.

Pen tips and other sharp objects can easily damage it.

The first thing you can do is gather a toolkit for your pyrography ventures. If you're new to that type of art, you should start with a simple beginner kit. The wood-burning method resembles a soldering iron with a hotter edge.

If you buy the whole kit, you'll get everything you need to get started. However, if you just purchase the instrument, you may need a set of tips. You'll also need sandpaper and a pair of needle-nose pinches. To put printed images on your wood, keep some black carbon tracing paper on hand.

For hot tips, pencils, erasers, respirators, electric fans and heat-resistant gloves, you'll also need a ceramic mug. If you want to finish the surface of your finished art piece, you can buy suitable transparent lacquer, varnish or wood stains.

CHAPTER 8

How To Work With Woodgrain In Your Woodburning Pyrography

The quality of the wood grain will make or break your fire. I first made a name for myself in pyrography by integrating grain into my designs. To help my realistic pictures, I used prominent grain to create a secondary pattern. It was a fun and thrilling equilibrium that straddled the realism-abstraction divide.

I'll show you how to work with the woodgrain in your woodburning in this chapter. There are two reasons why knowing how to work with the woodgrain in your burnings is significant. To begin with, working "against the grain" can cause you more problems than is required.

Second, ignoring grain patterns or selecting a wood with little grain is equivalent to throwing money away. Wood patterns can improve your work and are an advantage, not a liability when working with wood.

Understanding how to use woodgrain to improve your work without sabotaging is the secret to learning how to work with it in your woodburning. So, in this chapter, I'll give you some basic guidelines to help you get started.

Grain Patterns That Prevail

When dominant grain is woven into the artwork, it will improve your burnings. This does not imply that you build a template out of the grain but use the grain's movement to support the composition. The best way to do this is to make horizons, skies and water out of horizontal grain patterns.

The grain is one of my favorite things to use for birds in flight. I consider the grain to be air currents and integrate their placement in my composition with how the wings move the air.

Grain can also reinforce and echoes markings or patterns like stripes, making a burning even more effective. I also make new designs based on wood patterns. I always say that the wood chooses to look for you - and that's what I mean!

Next time you look at a dominant grain wood, let your mind go wild and develop some innovative ideas.

Grain Patterns

Even wood without a perceptible pattern will affect your work. Changes in the strength or softness of the components may cause a difference in burn density. Keep an eye on these events when putting your design around any vulnerable areas. I'm still double-checking the clear grain eye area so I don't have to fight for a smooth wood finish.

Converging lines are grain patterns that, due to optical illusion, can influence the final appearance of your work. A nose pressed against a vertical line of grain can seem pressed against something.

This is called a convergent line. These convergent lines are used to communicate the start and endpoints of the objects in perspective. Still, an unintended collide may produce a secondary illusion that interferes with the visual effect you try to achieve.

Fortunately, this is a simple problem to overcome. If you put your pattern on the wood, just compensate it slightly if you come up against a heavy grain line. The problem can be solved simply by overlapping or constructing a hole.

Knot holes have many the same problems. Keep an eye out for them so that they are not obscured in unintended places so that a secondary pattern can take over your composition. When the finish is applied, these seemingly insignificant patterns become more apparent (at which time it is too late to do anything).Ddirectional grain Patterns

Grain or patterns that run in a certain direction will explicitly contradict your image in some compositions. An example of this is the burning of an ocean sunset on the vertical grain. Instead, the vertical pattern contrasts the horizontal composition's tranquility with the water and horizon's heavy horizontal focus. It's not going to ruin the job but divert people from it.

It happened to me with reflective water recently, which prompted me to write this post. When very simple indications crossed the waterway at an angle, a secondary 'reflection' was produced that was inconsistent with the picture.

I couldn't change the orientation because it was a commissioned piece on the wood of the customer. The customer was approached and informed that I will continue the project independently. The customer was pleased because of my mixed feelings about the result. This only shows that even though you breach the rules, you still can have a satisfactory burn.

And now you know how to use wood grain on a basic level in your woodburning. This chapter does not try to deter you but helps you understand the advantages and disadvantages of working with the grain. Finally, the innovative use of grain will distinguish you from the competition. Enable your imagination to run wild for a new burning adventure.

CHAPTER 9

How Do You Get Pyrography Started?

To begin pyrography or wood-burning, you must first learn how to do the following:

- Gather all the appropriate materials.
- Select and prepare your wood.
- Build a prototype based on your preferences.
- Customize the design

There is a lot to learn about both of these areas to understand how to practice pyrography. When you learn more, you will be able to start your first wood-burning project.

Gather the required materials.

There isn't a lot of pyrography equipment or materials needed. The following is a list of the essential things you'll need:

• Printed Template • Tape • Sand Paper • Wood Burning Plumage • Carbon or Paper Graphite

Get your hands on the Wood Burning Pen Tool.

Set of wood-burning tools, including a pen and tips

The construction of a wood-burning plumber or wood burner is simple and soldering iron. The best stylus handles are heat-resistant and the handle is built to stay cool when keeping the tool. A heated metal element is included in the pen. Depending on the lines and styles you choose, you apply different tips to your pen.

When you're writing, the pen has protection between the handle and the metal to protect your fingers from burning. Wood burners usually come with a metal stand that you set up to keep the work surface from being burned and avoid a fire hazard.

Wood styles are available for purchase on the internet, in hobby stores and woodworking shops. They're not hard to come by. They are typically sold in packages that include various tips and other accessories, such as stencils.

You handle the wood burner in the same way you would a regular crayon to use it. To avoid burning your fingertips, keep your fingers above the guard. You'll find the most comfortable grip when you use the tool more.

The price of a wood burner can vary from less than $20 to hundreds of dollars. You can only switch them off or on with the cheapest choices, which typically don't have a temperature control feature.

The sun is uncontrollable. On the other hand, a temperature control system allows you to control the temperature of fire precisely. You'll pay a little extra, with the cheapest options costing about $40.

Imaginative Versa Method Walnut Hollow Vector

The majority of experts agree that if you spend a little more time controlling the pen's temperature. Since softwood is so hot, it makes learning the craft easier. You can use the tips to make different lines and patterns on the wood.

The tip screws or clicks into the wooden type's end. Each one is unique in terms of design or form. Some suggestions also include burning letters in the shape of a brand to make letter production easier.

Select the wood

The next step is to choose your wood. You can use almost any kind of wood but some types are better for beginners than others.

You want a block of wood with a light grain. The best way to make the burning look beautiful is to use a light woodblock, as darker wood makes it more difficult to see your work. The best woods are poplar, birchwood and basswood.

You can use hardwood but it is more difficult to burn and needs a higher fire. When compared to hardwood, you might expect to spend more time working on softwood. Perhaps this isn't the best place to start. You may also use scrap wood but never wood that has been finished. When you start to smoke, this poses a health risk.

Since you need a new piece for each project, this is probably the most expensive supply you'll need. However, you might obtain free wood from nature or inexpensive scrap parts from a wood yard. Smaller pieces of thinner wood purchased in bulk can save money, particularly early on.

WOODEN CIRCLES CRAFTS

A versatile wood piece is ideal for DIY projects and parties.

Smooth Surface: The wood's unfinished surface makes a painting, wood polishing and other finishing techniques simple.

Preparing the Wood

It is advisable to not attempt to start burning on a piece of wood before preparing. Working on a smooth and even surface is easier when you prepare your wood. This supports the production of good lines. Your wood needs to be sanded. It would help if you sanded it until it's fully smooth.

As you work, I strongly advise you progressively moving to finer sandpaper. As a result, any finer grain removes the scratches from the previous grain. If you think that sanding the grain makes your project work better, you can do so. Keep in mind that grain is easier to burn, so use it as much as possible in your design.

Remember, you can't use finished wood. However, if you have a painting piece, you can use it to sand away all the paint. You could skip this step if you bought prepared wood from a craft store because it's already smooth. There should also be no grain issues to consider.

Select a design template.

Before you start your wood-burning project, you must first decide what you want to create. Pyrograph designs are available for free or for purchase. You can also build your patterns.

If you're good at drawing, you can do anything you want with them. You can create them on your computer or even use an image as a starting point for your design. For this style, you print them out or remove them from the pattern book and convert them to wood with graphite or carbon paper.

The following are the steps you will take:

- Cut the wood graphite or carbon paper (200-pack) into shape.

- Place the template paper on the graphite paper.

- Using a tool or a pen, trace the template lines

- Remove all documents

One thing to keep in mind is that graphite paper has a darker side. The graphite is transferred to the wood by the darker side of the wood. You could add some pressure to the prototype to prevent it from going down. However, be vigilant when choosing a tool because you don't want anything sharp to rip the paper, tracing more difficult or damaging the wood.

Stencils for other craft applications are another way to develop your template. You'll need a regular crayon to draw the stencil on your wood. Holding and burning the stencil isn't necessary. This can damage the stencil and trigger burns on your hands.

When it comes to the first design, please keep it simple and straightforward. Black and white designs are the best because they don't need any additional coloring. Make sure the pattern size is appropriate for your piece of wood.

Burning Initiative

You're ready to start burning now that you've gathered all of your materials, chosen your wood, assembled it and transferred a template to it. If your wood burner has a temperature sensor, you can turn it on and adjust the temperature. The temperature you use is determined by the type of wood you use. Hardwood requires less heat and softwood requires more heat.

Before you start your project, you can practice on a piece of wood. It is possible to verify the temperature environment. You may also measure how easy it is to shift the style and how much pressure you use when using the wood burner. It also gives you the option of making mistakes.

On a piece of wood, it's much easier to make a mistake or do something incorrectly than it is on your project. When you're ready to begin working on your idea, the first move is to trace the design lines. All you need to do is cross all the lines. If your design has shading or integrates shading, don't think about it.

Hold the pen firmly in your hand and slowly direct it over the wood. For the best performance, keep your hand steady and continue to step. The deeper and darker the spot gets the longer the wood burner is left in one place. Slowly moving will help you avoid too thick or too dark ropes, deep grooves and lines, as you want your lines to be straight and even.

After you've traced all the lines, you can start filling in the gaps with shading and other information. Work slowly and keep your hand still. Shading is specialized information beyond the scope of this chapter but you can learn more about it here. If you learn better by watching someone demonstrate, you'll find this video helpful when you launch your first pyrography project.

CHAPTER 10

Pyrography Projects For Beginners

This chapter will show you how to test and approach your woodburning of these wonderful creatures using some techniques and parameters. Understanding how to analyze the method is critical because patterns may often remain when surfaces change dramatically. So, in this chapter, I'll show you three different ways to imagine these holes in your burnings.

Techniques and Equipment

Using different techniques for different areas is a simple way to explain different textures. A distinct final appearance can be achieved by combining smooth shading on one surface with a stippling underlay on another.

Remember that pyrography has the added benefit of allowing us to engrave textures. There is no texture when an area is mostly smooth shaded. Because of the shading on wood's reflective nature, it will appear glass-like and smooth in fact.

Since stippling does not absorb light in the same way as shading does, the effect becomes denser when you use it. Even though the pattern remains the same, this provides an entirely different look.

Changing pens is another way to ensure that two adjacent places have separate personalities. You may use a shader for the head and feet and a writer or skew for the shell. Using various pens or methods will help maintain the patterning but change the texture of your final fire.

Most texture changes would involve both an alternate technique and the use of a pen, so feel free to play with various combinations that look and feel good to you.

Intensity and Contrast

As we discussed in the first part, your artwork's physical texture will affect how light bounces off it. You may also look at your comparison to see if the intensity and contrast of different surfaces are different. I noticed that the markings' contrast and intensity were higher on the body's leathery portion than on the heavily textured shell in many of the reference photos.

As a result, I'll burn the skin with a wider spectrum of values (lights and darks) than the shell. For example, I'll use my darkest darks and lightest lights on the head markings but only darkest darks and medium lights on the shell (keeping my whites to a bare minimum). Keeping the strength and contrast of these elements under control helps keep the illusion of multiple surfaces alive.

Reflection Consistency

Last but not least, the reflective qualities of the paint. As I stated briefly in the previous section under technique, smooth surfaces reflect light more than rough and pitted surfaces. It is often appropriate for an artist to slightly exaggerate this quality to connect visually with the viewer.

Make the rough areas slightly rougher and the smooth areas slightly smoother to put it another way. This is, without a doubt, a stretch of the imagination. No, you're not "photographic" anymore.

If you don't have the meaning range of an image to begin with, you can't be photographic - pyrographers who achieve the illusion are highly skilled at knowing what to capture and what to leave behind.

Don't be fooled: understanding this art form's strengths and weaknesses is essential for creating high-quality work. Pyrography is a luscious, rich medium that communicates beauty in a way that no other medium can. These ideas will help you create images that captivate the viewer's attention and represent your subject's enthusiasm.

How To Burn Necks And Chins

When it comes to portraits, necks are a common stumbling block for most artists. The division between the head and neck is also simplified by drawing a straight line. And if this line isn't placed right and an EXACT form, the whole image would appear uncomfortable and unrealistic.

Why do we feel compelled to do so? Becuase our brains tell us to!

When you were a child, you separated the head (which was an oval) from the neck (two parallel lines) to represent the head and neck. It's suitable for a boy and a strong symbolic representation of the head and neck, a fairly universal representation.

However, when moving to realism, symbolism must be discarded. You need to learn not only to see but also to understand the structure of your subject matter. This isn't nearly as complicated as it seems. It's a lot of fun and exciting. It will make you more aware of the beauty that surrounds you.

This is probably why I love art so much. It motivates me to learn more and rewards me for my curiosity.

Even though we're addressing chins and necks, I hope this will help you become more aware of other places where similar situations occur to develop not only your burnings but also your observation skills.

Shapes and Principles

Necks are the transition points between two planes. Unlike a box, there are no sharp edges. Instead, we're dealing with convex and concave surfaces that gently undulate at times and harshly at others, casting shadows that match their form.

How To Woodburn Realistic Fur

There is a popular misconception in the woodburning community that there is only one way to burn fur. Unfortunately, this misunderstanding leads to mediocre results in almost any attempt to make a practical burning.

What is the explanation for this? Because you are not attempting to burn fur! You're destroying the appearance of fur

What is the fur illusion?

Value (lights and darks), texture (line quality) and contour combine to create the illusion of fur (line direction).

These three concepts would go a long way toward explaining how to burn realistically and adapt your technique to produce beautiful fur consistently.

I'll clarify these three concepts and how to apply them to your burnings in this section.

The difference between lights and darks is known as value. This disparity can be measured in two ways: the overall image's lightness and darkness and the lightness and darkness of the area immediately adjacent to the portion you're burning.

It's crucial to comprehend the overall value palette you're dealing with to achieve a clean and crisp burn. It's quick to overestimate your beliefs if you compare your lights and darks to what's right next to them.

When placed next to unburned wood, any value will appear dark. If a value is next to a fully black line, it will appear bright. When assessing your burning, keep this in mind.

This is why certain pyrographers would burn a dark backdrop at the start of their work to ensure that they have a precise description of Whitest White and Blackest Black. This makes it easier to grasp and control your middle tones.

However, not all burning would look good against a dark backdrop. While this technique can look dramatic, overusing it can result in the cliched "painting on velvet" look of the 1970s.

Don't get me wrong: it's an important tactic. Only remember not to use it as a crutch.

To make realistic fur, you must be able to control the lightness or darkness of the fur you're burning, both overall and concerning the environment immediately surrounding it. When most of us think of fur, we think of this. The line quality you use to build this illusion will make or break the overall look.

What kind of fur are you smoldering?

How does it make you feel?

Is it fine and gentle or rough and heavy?

Some lines are stronger than others. A short, dark, straight stroke would appear spikier than a short, medium, slightly curved stroke. The contrast between the two is striking. I advise students to "sense" their way through the correct stroke with their pens. Many people prefer to press down too hard on the pen, resulting in a thick, rigid line

Pretend you're stroking the animal you're burning to reach the best line efficiency. If it's a soft and delicate rabbit, use soft and delicate strokes. This means you'll have a distinct feel and pace than if you're digging into a bison's coarse neck fur. By "feeling" your way through the fur, you send a signal to your brain to change your touch.

Contour

The final theory to consider is contour. Contour creates a three-dimensional look for your picture, which is referred to as shape. You can master the illusion of realism by changing the direction and duration of the fur burn.

Examine your reference to ensure that your strokes are in the correct direction and are the correct duration. Avoid the temptation to "cheat" by using longer strokes to finish faster.

This will detract from your work's overall appearance because you'll have to go back in and fix the strokes again when you remember they're not right, extending the time it takes to complete.

And there you have it: my three rules for producing realistic-looking fur! Take this into account as you analyze your subject and change your burning to show the illusion you want to make.

The Art of Drawing Dogs on Wood

Drawing animals, especially dogs, is enjoyable and satisfying. This is a fantastic trick to master. Pyrography is the art of burning images onto wood and it's a technique I like to use. Pyrography has existed for millennia.

You can either create your laser pen or purchase one. I prefer to use a soldering device or, to put it another way, a soldering pencil. Since dogs are my passion, I typically draw them or something related to them. I took a very big desk drawer and cut a square hole in it, making sure the square hole was centered and even.

Then I glued only the edges of a window glass over the square hole to create a glass window in the once-large cabinet. Then I rigged a light fixture on the inside of the drawer so you could turn it upside down and lay your picture or whatever image you wanted to burn to the wood on top of it.

I enjoy seeing photographs of dogs. You can now copy something with the tracer light. Place the picture on top of the bottle. Place a piece of paper on top of the picture and square it up against the mirror. Turn on the light and trace your copy of the photograph.

You now have a disposable copy of the photograph. Now you can place the copy you made on top of the wood you chose to burn your image on. Place it where you want it and protect it to prevent it from moving.

But first and most importantly, put a piece of carbon paper underneath the copy of the Dog photo you made and then draw or trace the lines of the copy of the Dog photo you made. Remove everything from the wood and begin burning the lines that the carbon paper left behind.

How to Make The Walking Stick Exclusive

The first and most obvious choice is to engrave a plaque on a walking stick. A silver or brass collar or a wider area such as the handle maybe engraved on certain walking sticks. On a collar, there is enough room to write a name, initials or a date. If engraving the collar is too complicated, a brass plaque can be engraved and tacked to the shaft instead.

A plaque gives you a little more room to add a name and a date and a note or a short saying. The plaques themselves may be silver-plated or brass and can be bent around the shaft in any form. Pennies may also be used.

Many people want to decorate their walking sticks with badges. The badges are bent around the shaft of the stick once more before being glued or tacked on. British counties, teams, national flags football clubs, military badges cats, horses, Celtic or other symbols are all available on the market today.

There are also popular people, sites and animals to be found. The pewter badges are much attractive and the other badges are typically very colorful and give your cane many personalities.

Straps, ribbons and other items tied around the handle and whistles give a walking stick some personality. You may use a dog whistle or a duck call to call your cat. Whistles are often tied around the shaft or inserted into the handle. For instance, a V-shaped thumbstick with a whistle carved into one of the tines.

Another choice for customizing a walking stick is to have the handle carved out of wood or made out of resin in the shape of your pet's head. You might, for example, have a black labrador head with your pet's name painted on the collar. Resin is a wonderful substance that can be rendered to look like the real thing by pouring it into a mold and then painting it.

Pyrography is another beautiful art form that looks fantastic on a walking stick. Pyrography is burning a pattern into the wood with a special pen that resembles a soldering iron. With this approach, you can get some thorough and lovely results.

CHAPTER 11

How to Become An Expert Pyrographer

You would be able to burn something at any time if you have three elements. Since mastering them provides a high degree of comprehension, I refer to them as the Ph.D. of pyrography. These three controls can be used to troubleshoot and solve any burning problems you can encounter.

These three elements are crucial because they regulate your line's quality based on the pyrographic method, which is unique among art mediums.

I'll clarify what they are, how they function and when you can use them in this post. The letters Ph.D. stand for Strain, Heat and Length. As a result, learning and understanding how to use them give you a superior ability to troubleshoot intelligently and solve problems quickly.

The letter P stands for PRESSURE

The first factor is the amount of strain. You can get a darker burn by applying more pressure. This also helps you to engrave on the wood's surface to add depth. A lighter burn mark can result from lowering your pressure. Pressure helps you to quickly change your burns without wasting time turning up or down the heat.

Pressure will offer your artwork fascinating textures and subtleties that are difficult to achieve with other two-dimensional mediums.

The letter H stands for HEAT

It may seem self-evident that more heat equals a darker burn and less heat equals a lighter burn but it's worth repeating. As we mentioned in the previous lesson, adjusting your heat depending on what you're working on will help you maintain a relaxed rhythm.

Remembering that your comfort level is directly proportional to your control level when burning can help you understand when to use this feature instead of others to troubleshoot and correct.

If you have a sensitive area in your design that needs precision, lowering the heat allows you to better position your pen and make adjustments if necessary. When working on eyes, I use this a lot because I know that any deviation will radically alter the artwork.

The letter D stands for DURATION

The easiest change made for your burning is to increase the time or intensity. The longer your pen is on the wood, the darker the burn will be because it is the heat that is doing the work.

This is the most important shading theory. You can maintain a smooth and steady rhythm without having to wait for your tool to heat up or cool down by slowing down in the darker areas and speeding up in the lighter areas.

This is an excellent aspect to modify when working with grain or soft/resistant soil areas. If you find that you're hitting a soft spot, simply speed up your stroke when you get to that segment. Slow down in hard/resistant areas to allow your tool to do its job properly. This will give your burning a uniform appearance.

Furthermore, when burning on wood with a skew, particularly when working with animal fur or feathers, burning parallel to the grain can be difficult. Your skew's blade will sink into the grain, resulting in a darker burn. And if you sink in, using a quicker pace will keep your burns consistent.

Congratulations on your achievement! You've earned your Ph.D. in Pyrography! And now, just like any Ph.D., it's time to bring what you've learned into effect. Find a basic pattern and experiment with each variable to see what the variations are. You will find that you need to combine one or more of these elements to burn what you want successfully.

Understanding these three elements gives you the ability to approach your work with confidence because you know the physics of what's going on and how to manage it. These elements may not make your job simpler or quicker but they will help you make the choices you need to burn effectively on any surface.

CHAPTER 12

Ideas For A First Move To Learn Pyrography

1. What should your first move be if you want to learn Pyrography or the art of wood-burning?

To begin, familiarize yourself by reading books from your local library or conducting internet research. Take a look at the job that Pyrographers do. Learn about the various Pyrography machines and equipment available for purchase and the results that can be accomplished with them.

When looking for Pyrographic tool manufacturers, take a look at the variety of ready-made items you can purchase to make your products.

2. When I first started Pyrography, I quickly discovered that woods containing resin, such as pine, would emit toxic fumes when burned. The

acrid odor got stuck in the back of my throat and made me cough.

After reading about wood toxicity, I realized that wearing a mask is important when burning woods with resin or painted and sealed with lacquers and woods that have been treated with chemicals. Act in a well-ventilated area at all times.

3. When it comes to burning materials, the best and simplest solution for Pyrography is to buy your wooden blanks from a Pyrographic supplier, who can guarantee their accuracy and suitability for wood burning.

Woods like beech, sycamore, lime and high-quality plywood are available from a Pyrographic supplier. Another choice is to purchase wood from a dealer specializing in supplying raw timber to furniture makers and woodturners. I was fortunate enough to come across a nearby woodturning center to buy wood from various sources.

Some of these woods had some surfaces to burn on, with varying densities and widths of graining. Be wary of Pyrography issues that may arise from uneven burning, as the wood's grain affects the intensity and pace at which your tool burns the wood's surface. It is preferable to use close-grained hardwood if you want an even impact.

4. If this is your first time doing Pyrography, I recommend keeping your design simply because the result will be more successful. Try tracing around a drinks coaster or an upturned glass with a soft pencil or drawing a basic flower shape to find something with a simple and easily recognizable outline.

Next, try burning it onto a piece of wood with a ball-style nib, which will allow you to build the curve of your shape more easily. For example, selecting a slightly more complicated form - a shape with corners - might be the next move.

Learn as many outlines as you can and once you've mastered creating a clean-cut line, you'll be able to make a basic outline template to paint. Choose from a range of materials to color your shapes, including acrylic paints and watercolor, felt tip pens and markers.

5. Make your test woods out of scraps by making a series of graded marks and various patterns with various contact intensities. Use these test woods as a guide and you'll be able to tackle larger Pyrography projects in no time.

6. Pyrography is a 'Fire Art,' and the fire must be controlled; your protection is just as vital as anyone else's; please do not be reckless or take dangerous shortcuts; it is not worth it!

Always switch off your computer when not in use and never leave a machine turned on unattended; it's always safer to be safe than sorry! If you leave other materials too close to the machine and catch fire, it will only take seconds for the fire to spread, so be careful!

7. Once you've learned the fundamentals of pyrography, there are many possibilities open to you. You may make presents for your friends or small pieces of art to sell at a stall to raise money for a charity, for example. Pyrography also allows everyone the ability to start their own company if they so desire.

Wood burning supplies catalogs sell various simple wooden household goods such as boxes, spoons, picture frames and other items to burn patterns onto. The Pyrography picture will look more effective as a decoration on a household item of your choice if the design is plain.

Pyrography is a very enjoyable hobby, whether you want to explore it further and start a small business or just do it for fun. Whatever you want to do, be proud that you are contributing to the survival of an ancient craft but don't forget to tell others about it and inspire them to try it as well!

CHAPTER 13

Shapes To Assist You In Creating Your Designs

If you haven't read the previous chapters, please do so before reading this one to make more sense! We'll find out what you can do with your new resources in this chapter.

What are the tips and how do you use them?

Of course, there are a variety of options. The question is, which ones are essential to get going?

Do you want to concentrate specifically on shading?

What do you mean by broad lines?

Is it a mix?

That depends on what you're making and for whom you're making it. Making a large sign, for example, for a shop or advertisement, is an example.

You'll want a wide tip so you can quickly cover a large area. A tiny sign for your front porch, on the other hand, is a completely different story. Use a fine tip for prose and thicker lines (borders) or decorations, use a broad tip.

Here are some of the most helpful hints, whether you've already decided what you want to design or not.

Tapered Point: You'll want to sign your name on the front or back of your project with the fine tip of the tapered point. This is the tip that I find myself employing the most. It may draw straight or curved lines on various surfaces, write in cursive or block letters, and create intricate designs.

Shading Point: This tip is shaped like a bent "spear" and is one of the most flexible tips. Because of the point's form, it can hit places were other tips can't. With just a light touch, this tip produces beautiful shading.

Calligraphy Point: Using this tip, you can create eye-catching calligraphy lettering and shaping.

Flow Point: This rounded tip is great for drawing large lines (curved or straight), writing and dotting or shading dots.

There are a few others that are accessible but aren't used as frequently:

Hot knife Point: Can cut and shape a variety of materials, including cork, plastic and gourds, also to wood.

Color and black-and-white laser copy images are transferred to some surfaces using the Transfer Stage. Transferring complicated patterns is a breeze with this method.

There is also a range of shapes to choose from to assist you in creating your designs. Stars, triangles, circles and other geometric shapes are examples. You can use any combination of these for any medium you like.

CHAPTER 14

How To Find Inspirational Ideas For Pyrography Projects

How do you come up with fresh Pyrographic ideas when your mind goes blank and all imagination has dried up? Don't put too much pressure on yourself!

Take Note: A strong dose of relaxation accompanied by a little exercise will help loosen up the thought waves. Give yourself some time to relax and do nothing strenuous, such as taking a relaxing bath or lounging in a super-comfy spot while reading a good book! If you can get out in the fresh air later, do some light physical exercise - a half-hour walk will suffice - and then return to base.

1. First and foremost, get yourself into a nice relaxing room on your own and enjoy doing a mind-clearing exercise - and no, I'm not talking about

push-ups! For the time being, Pyrography is a no-no!

2. Make a list of a few similar word pairs, including those describing emotions and writing them down on a piece of paper. Make sure there's enough room underneath the words to draw a simple symbol to represent each one.

Are you up for it?

Have some colored pencils on hand and as you read through your paired words, quickly draw symbols that represent your pair of words (don't overthink it; just do it); draw whatever comes to mind from your fingertips with a colored pencil of your choice!

Let's look at the word pair examples below and then come up with your own.

Light vs. Dark: Good vs. Sad: Ground vs. Sea

Home - Away: Black - White: Cool - Furious: Black - White: Home - Away

Big vs. Small: Hot vs. Cold: Beautiful vs. Unattractive:

CHAPTER 14

How To Find Inspirational Ideas For Pyrography Projects

How do you come up with fresh Pyrographic ideas when your mind goes blank and all imagination has dried up? Don't put too much pressure on yourself!

Take Note: A strong dose of relaxation accompanied by a little exercise will help loosen up the thought waves. Give yourself some time to relax and do nothing strenuous, such as taking a relaxing bath or lounging in a super-comfy spot while reading a good book! If you can get out in the fresh air later, do some light physical exercise - a half-hour walk will suffice - and then return to base.

1. First and foremost, get yourself into a nice relaxing room on your own and enjoy doing a mind-clearing exercise - and no, I'm not talking about

push-ups! For the time being, Pyrography is a no-no!

2. Make a list of a few similar word pairs, including those describing emotions and writing them down on a piece of paper. Make sure there's enough room underneath the words to draw a simple symbol to represent each one.

Are you up for it?

Have some colored pencils on hand and as you read through your paired words, quickly draw symbols that represent your pair of words (don't overthink it; just do it); draw whatever comes to mind from your fingertips with a colored pencil of your choice!

Let's look at the word pair examples below and then come up with your own.

Light vs. Dark: Good vs. Sad: Ground vs. Sea

Home - Away: Black - White: Cool - Furious: Black - White: Home - Away

Big vs. Small: Hot vs. Cold: Beautiful vs. Unattractive:

Sun vs. Moon: Young vs. Old: Liquid vs. Solid

Long vs. short: day vs. night: loud vs. quiet: long vs. short: long vs. short: long vs. short: long vs. short: long vs. short: long vs. short: long vs. short

Mountain - Valley: Love-Hate: Laugh - Cry:

For you, was this a fun little experiment?

Now choose a few of your favorite tunes. Choose three or four discs that cover a wide variety of musical styles, such as blues, rock, non-serious classical, folk and so on. Switch on the radio if you don't have enough coverage at home.

Play a track of each music piece and draw shapes and symbols that come to mind due to the rhythm and sounds you've chosen as you listen.

I listen to a wide variety of music and one of my CDs features African rhythms. When I play it, images reflecting the continent's strong hot colors always seem to appear for me. So pick carefully and listen to a selection of interesting sounds to pique your interest.

So, now that you've scribbled something down, how do you feel?

a) Experiment further by writing a list of matching words for each of your pairs of terms on a separate piece of paper.

Or

b) Choose a soothing piece of music, close your eyes and listen intently, only opening your eyes to jot down ideas that match the sounds you're hearing. Your mind/imagination should now be free to translate the words or sounds of music into patterns or designs you can use in your Pyrography.

If you're having trouble coming up with a pair of terms that piques your interest, repeat the exercise using words from a thesaurus. Try borrowing something completely different from your local library than what you normally listen to (ethnic music, classical music or a CD with improvisational sounds, for example). Listen to music that you would not normally listen to.

Some CDs are naturally inspired, including sounds from the rainforest, oceans, earth, wind and animal sounds such as dolphins, whales, birds, and so on, if you want to listen to sounds that have a natural feel. Use these to activate your senses and construct beautiful Pyrography that is special to you.

Don't be too set in your ways; stretch your Pyrography boundaries and try things you've never done before. Using your senses in new ways can be liberating and thrilling and you might end up with some unexpected and inspiring Pyrography!

Visiting a gallery or craft center is always a worthwhile and enjoyable activity for soaking up ideas that you can interpret in your unique way and use to create your own Pyrography.

Let me state right away that you should not be thinking about copying someone else's work but rather considering alternative crafts to Pyrography. Examine the design, color and presentation of each craft.

A student will always be shown examples of work in any form of education. It's sometimes helpful to show good and bad examples so that a student can figure out what will work and what won't.

Seeing accomplished individuals' work provides the student with a benchmark of quality work to strive for and a wide range of workable ideas to draw from to stimulate their imagination and create quality Pyrography.

CHAPTER 15

Getting The Most Out Of A Day At An Arts And Crafts Show

If you get the chance to attend one of the larger Arts and Crafts Exhibitions, which include both craftsmen and suppliers of crafts materials, take advantage of it.

A feast of artist supplies and equipment and displays of work and demonstrations will greet you. You should observe masters of their various crafts at work and you may even have the opportunity to try out a new one. There will be chances to ask questions and receive expert advice.

Make the most of the resources available to you because they will be plentiful. Don't just wander around aimlessly in the exhibition. Make a few notes about what you want to get out of the day before you go.

Use bullet points to write down each of the important things you want to learn about for your Pyrography on a notepad and then use these points to jog your memory as you walk around the exhibition. When there are such a wide variety of things to see, it is easy to become distracted.

It's very convenient to have this type of hands-on experience all in one place. How often do you get the chance to be surrounded by such a diverse group of people and immersed in an exciting extravaganza of all things arts and crafts?

Take your time looking through the colorful materials and equipment on display by suppliers and you're sure to come up with new and innovative ideas to help you with your Pyrography. You might start to see how to present your work in a novel and creative way.

Is there anything in the exhibition that you find particularly stimulating as a piece of work as you walk around?

If so, what is it about this piece that draws you in?

Is it the final presentation of the entire piece or the design, colors and materials used?

You could jot down a few words representing the qualities that excite your imagination once you've narrowed down what you like about the art/craftwork. Consider modifying your Pyrography to include some of the same qualities that inspire you.

Due to the competition among craft suppliers, there will most likely be opportunities to purchase artists' materials/equipment at reduced prices and collect catalogs and website addresses for future use. Utilize free samples to help you remember their displays and use them as memory triggers.

Allow the day to help you loosen up your thoughts and allow your mind to consider your Pyrography craft from various perspectives. This relaxing and enjoyable experience can be used as an educational tool that, in the end, may lead to new and exciting opportunities for you!

CHAPTER 16

Small Pyrography Business Start-Up Suggestions

1. Make a clear schedule that includes the Pyrography objects you want to sell and the prices you hope to achieve. If you're unsure about the markup amount, consider how much you'd be willing to be paid every hour to do this job.

First, add the cost of the raw materials used to the equation: cost of materials + how many hours it took to make your piece of work (whatever you decide is a reasonable hourly rate of pay.) I suggest doing your research at craft fairs and other venues to see how your rivals price their work.

You won't know how long it took them to create their Pyrography but it should give you a good idea of whether your work would be overpriced or underpriced. Remember that your goal is to sell but don't undervalue the time and effort you put in.

2. Purchase a register to store all of your customer orders and letters (in date order) and a writing book with lined paper to keep track of your bank/building society account's daily transactions.

It's probably a smart idea to set up a separate account for your new Pyrography company so you can keep track of all incoming and outgoing expenses. Be sure to mark your new exercise/writing book with the account's name and number.

Draw four lines from the top of your book's first few pages to the bottom.

Label the first column [date], the second [+ credits], the third [- debits] and the fourth [balance]. For your [- debit column], use red ink. for the credit column and a black pen

Subtract the amount you've spent from the balance and enter the new number below. (I'm sure you already know this and you may think it's a waste of time to write it all down but remember it is far more difficult when you're busy; you may prefer to keep notes on your computer.)

Your book will help you provide any financial details needed for tax purposes once your company is up and running and maintaining your receipts for the same purpose; organize your receipts by date by stapling them together.

Keep track of all receipts attached to your Pyrography business, includes the following items: equipment (points, nibs masks, etc.), materials (cloth, wood paper, etc.) and colors (pens, paints, inks and varnishes).

3. Check off each transaction on your monthly statements to ensure they are correct. This can seem to be a hassle when you can easily call or look up details on the internet. Still, as a small Pyrography business owner, this strategy can keep you very aware of your expenditures daily. You will also be told of the sum of money that is available to you.

4. If you have rented a stall or are advertising your wares in a shop or on the internet, showing

Pyrography articles linked by design and color can be one of the best ways to get people's attention. It's necessary to make the exhibit stand out from the rest of the crowd.

For example, you can have three or four things with entirely different designs but all painted in different shades of blue. If you show your Pyrography work in a single color setting, you can create a striking display.

To set off your work, you might want to add a couple of items in a nice contrasting color. Another option is to use things with a similar theme that you may have borrowed or that are already in your home to improve your show simply!

5. If your Pyrography such as a decorated picture frame or a candle holder serves a secondary purpose, don't forget to illustrate its usefulness by showing it with a picture in it or a candle in the holder.

6. Consider re-decorating the old furniture. If you come across something you'd like to work with, this

could be a fun little project. It presents you with the exciting task of re-vamping and upgrading it with your own unique Pyrography theme. You could use your larger piece of furniture as a focal point for many smaller groups of household items that you've decorated yourself!

7. Here are some suggestions on where you can sell your work. Village fetes, coffee mornings at churches, car boots, school fetes, renting a market stall (which can be very affordable) or photographing your Pyrography and selling it on eBay are all possibilities.

You might approach small coffee shops or restaurants and ask if they'd be interested in displaying a selection of your work in exchange for a percentage of any sales.

Important: Make sure you market yourself as a Pyrography business. Ensure your business has a name that can be burned onto a customized signboard that you can display where you sell your work. Make your own Pyrography business cards and give them out at art shows and other activities. People will be able to take a couple from your table.

CHAPTER 17

Take Advantage Of Every Chance To Promote Your Pyrography Business

Place a themed advertisement in your local magazines, such as Christmas, Easter or birthdays. In my neighborhood, there is a new bus that makes stops in neighborhoods to broadcast live. They invite others to join them in conversation. This may be another way to advertise yourself and get more people interested in pyrography as a hobby.

1. Set yourself up at a craft fair or similar event where you can show your Pyrography and encourage the public to watch your work as soon as possible. (When it comes to vehicles, public safety always comes first.) If you want to engage the public in practical work, you'll need to perform a risk assessment.

If you have the room and the right machine/nibs, why not give the public members a chance to make a simple design?

They could burn their name on a wooden pendant or key ring fob for a small fee to cover your expenses. Inviting people to try their hand at Pyrography will pique people's interest in the art and inspire them to look at your for-sale pieces.

Take the time to explain the safety rules to each person clearly. Most importantly, make it clear that an adult must supervise all children and that any child wishing to try out Pyrography in a public space must be at least eight years old.

2. Create an ambiance for people visiting your show to draw and cater to your customers. Show quality examples of the various woods you use for Pyrography if you're burning on wood. You might come across a nice piece of wood in its natural states, such as a log or a portion of a log with oddly patterned bark.

Display it in a way that highlights the log's cut instead of similar-shaped objects you might have burned, such as a photo plaque. If you can gather a few leaves, cones or other tree products, arrange them in a natural yet appealing way around your display area.

Do you have a friend or know of someone who might record a creepy little tune for you on tape or disc, maybe with a flute or other complementary musical instrument?

You will find a spot on the internet where you can download public domain music without having to worry about copyright. Set up surround sound and play your disc to add to the wood-burning atmosphere but don't turn up the volume to the point that it drowns out anything else. Choose something that corresponds to your work's theme.

3. Use the art of Fascination to sow the seeds of lust in your audience. Increase interest in Pyrography by distributing teasers in which people can handle pieces of wood and guess what kind of wood it is and

a short sample wood map that allows them to figure out the answers for themselves.

If you want to take your quiz a step further, create a second chart with silhouettes of each tree form so that the public can compare the wood to a tree silhouette—link completing the quizzes and receiving a free wood-burning item.

4. Ensure you have a big enough sign to read from a distance and explain what the Art of Pyrography is all about. Create a folder with a list of the various types of products you use and their sources. If you just burn wood, you can use wood products from newly planted forests, so make sure you have a sign that encourages this and explains why.

On your show, have knowledge books about trees and wood in general. If you're worried they'll run away, use an easy-to-make slip-on cover with a tie to secure it to your display table.

5. Create a second folder to house a series of high-quality Pyrography images that aren't on display. Include a price list and a notice indicating that your

work can be ordered ahead of time. Offer a small personalized item as an enticement for placing an order with you.

6. Distribute freebies. Create some Pyrography freebies with your name and contact information written on the back that is simple to make and inexpensive (purchase a small stamp with your details on it for quick and easy use).

Create some card bookmarks and small gift cards and embellish them with a mounted design burned onto paper. You can choose from some colors for the card and a contrasting color for the paper to turn on.

Prepare a few basic designs for the paper pieces, such as a geometric pattern or flowers. You should be able to make them in the evening and then mount them on your bookmarks and cards when you next have a half-hour free. There's no need to do all these things at once; instead, choose a few of them to help draw people over to your stall or show area.

CHAPTER 18

Frequently Asked Questions

1. How do I determine the Pyrography equipment purchase?

If you've done your homework, you'll already know that the computers available for purchase are priced differently. I wanted a more inexpensive Janik pyrography computer as a beginner.

Janik makes some machines, some of which have a feature that allows you to choose from various nibs/points. These are simple to install on the computer and can help you achieve a variety of results. Peter Child also makes Pyrography machines with a variety of tool heads to complement Janik's.

2. Where can I get inexpensive wood to practice on?

Until I found a nearby woodturning supplier, I went to the hardware store and bought many pine pieces to practice Pyrography because they were cheap but remember to wear a mask if you do this. You can acquire rarer woods at a lower cost by buying old furniture but you must remove any lacquer or finish from the wood.

You'll either need to cut the wood down to a manageable size or hire someone to do it for you; ordinary paper is another inexpensive material to use.

I've tried burning primarily onto white paper and the amount of heat needed to achieve subtle sepia tones for a design is shocking. I was apprehensive when I first put my Pyrographic tool on the document, fearing that it would burst into flames! Why don't you give it a shot?

Start by setting your computer to the lowest setting and ensuring that your paper is placed on a flame-resistant surface.

3. What is the best way to create a professional Pyrography Design?

When I first started wood burning, I chose many basic patterns and images but I soon realized that these would not be considered works of art and themselves, as I wanted to take a more creative approach to my Pyrography.

A good craft supplier should advise you on the methods you should use to move a picture onto your wood if you intend to sell simple items with a Pyrographic decoration. You don't need to draw to create your patterns and designs using tracing paper and templates.

Visit a few art supplies stores and take your time looking at what they have to offer. Create a list of what you may want to purchase at a later date. With practice, your Pyrography will look more professional in no time.

4. I'd like to add some color to my Pyrography. What should I do?

Coloring supplies are readily available and reasonably priced in craft stores. To color in your Pyrography designs, you can choose from a range of pens and pencils. Water-based felt tips blend well and allow you to see the wood's surface better than permanent markers or felt tip pens.

You can make a softer and gentler variety of colors with pencil crayons. Often try out acrylics, watercolor inks, pencils, wood stains and felt-tipped pens on a small same wood piece before using them on a larger piece. This way, before you color your Pyrography, you can see the impact you'll get.

5. How do I professionally show my Pyrography?

You can purchase acrylic lacquer or fixatives to spray your work with and pick between a natural matt or a highly polished finish. You may choose to use an oil such as Danish Oil or wax such as Beeswax; however, these products may darken the color of the wood while also bringing out the grain, which is perfect for wood art.

Working with wood in this particular way opens up a world of possibilities for the imagination to run wild. With practice, you can improve your skills, allowing you to create a delicate and reliable and professional Pyrography, appealing to a wider audience.

Pyrography is fun and ancient art that I would recommend everyone to try. Its design helps you create a good piece of 'Fire Art' work with little or no drawing ability and it is a very rewarding way to spend a few spare hours during the week. You'll also be helping to keep Pyrography alive as an old craft and who knows, you may decide to make it more than just a passing interest!

CHAPTER 19

Tips To Make A Fortune Out Of Your Pyrography Art Passion

If you live and breathe Pyrography or whatever your passion is, you'll still be on the lookout for new possibilities and you'll make time to practice and improve your Pyrography on most days.

When you first start your small Pyrography business, it will not automatically make you wealthy. If you want to give yourself the best chance to be highly skilled and ultimately make Pyrography your profession, you must be willing to keep learning whenever you have free time from your regular day job.

The more enthusiastic you are about Pyrography, the more credible you will appear and the more respected you will be, particularly if you have worked hard to master your craft. If you are information and helpful tips and advice on where to purchase Pyrography tools, blanks and materials at fair prices. In that case, you are likely to pique their interest.

If you pique the interest of arts/crafts enthusiasts, you may be able to convince them to approach you and ask if you would be willing to teach them Pyrography for a fair fee. Make some flyers to encourage one-on-one lessons or small workshops. In terms of the place for your classes, you must be prepared.

It could be in your own home if you set up a secure working space, have spare equipment and materials on hand and have a clear idea of many planned lessons that start from the beginning. Remember to factor in the cost of practice supplies, energy, and ancillary things when calculating your teaching cost.

If you are enthusiastic about what you are doing, it will rub off on your students and they will spread the word about your abilities and enthusiasm for pyrography. You would be able to get bookings for

passionate about something, whether it
Pyrography or any art or hobby, you would not f
obligated to work in a certain way.

Your excitement will motivate you to try out n
techniques in your profession. For example, y
could create a line of Pyrography items with
nostalgic feel to them or if you're creative, you co
create a line of your abstract designs;
possibilities are endless.

Start with the basics and advertise your Pyrogra
locally; once you've identified yourself as an ex]
you can extend your field of work nationally
internationally if you so desire.

When talking to potential buyers or showing
Pyrography at local galleries and craft venue
curiosity and education, the more excitement
knowledge you can bring into your discussion;
the more planning and preparation you put
your displays, the more likely you are to make a

Suppose you are willing to donate any of your
time to support others by offering free Pyrog

information and helpful tips and advice on where to purchase Pyrography tools, blanks and materials at fair prices. In that case, you are likely to pique their interest.

If you pique the interest of arts/crafts enthusiasts, you may be able to convince them to approach you and ask if you would be willing to teach them Pyrography for a fair fee. Make some flyers to encourage one-on-one lessons or small workshops. In terms of the place for your classes, you must be prepared.

It could be in your own home if you set up a secure working space, have spare equipment and materials on hand and have a clear idea of many planned lessons that start from the beginning. Remember to factor in the cost of practice supplies, energy, and ancillary things when calculating your teaching cost.

If you are enthusiastic about what you are doing, it will rub off on your students and they will spread the word about your abilities and enthusiasm for pyrography. You would be able to get bookings for passionate about something, whether it is Pyrography or any art or hobby, you would not feel obligated to work in a certain way.

Your excitement will motivate you to try out new techniques in your profession. For example, you could create a line of Pyrography items with a nostalgic feel to them or if you're creative, you could create a line of your abstract designs; the possibilities are endless.

Start with the basics and advertise your Pyrography locally; once you've identified yourself as an expert, you can extend your field of work nationally and internationally if you so desire.

When talking to potential buyers or showing your Pyrography at local galleries and craft venues for curiosity and education, the more excitement and knowledge you can bring into your discussions and the more planning and preparation you put into your displays, the more likely you are to make a sale.

Suppose you are willing to donate any of your spare time to support others by offering free Pyrography small talks and demonstrations at community events, for example.

It's also helpful to build connections to pyrography sites on the internet and have your website. If you are not familiar with computer technology, try engaging with woodwork professionals such as woodburners and furniture makers in person. You will collaborate and encourage your crafts and skills, leading to opportunities to use your decorative arts in ways you had not considered previously.

1. Keep it easy at first and begin by making Pyrography pieces that you are familiar with. Do what you know best. Producing a stock of your Pyrographic work to sell will seem overwhelming at first but if you start with simple products that do not require a lot of complex decoration, you can quickly build up a reserve to sell.

Since you want to show basic Pyrography objects, you should have no trouble reproducing them in the future if you are asked to construct a similar item with a personalized theme or to highlight it in a different color.

Simplicity will make a difference and assist you in dealing with additional Pyrography orders. You will have the expertise and trust to schedule the collection of the finished product from the customer.

2. It's time to make a decision - what makes you tick and gives you a buzz?

After you've mastered the simpler pieces of Pyrography, you can begin to add and develop your set of more complex pieces of work that are reasonably priced - (never forget to time how long a piece of Pyrography takes from start to finish, so that you can always mark it up at a suitable price).

When you're wood burning, consider what types of projects bring you the most pleasure and happiness when they're done - in other words, what is your Burning Passion?

Note, these are your first steps in pyrography or fire art and if you're starting a Pyrography business, you'll need to think about how you want your business to expand. If you enjoy and get a buzz from creating products with lettering/calligraphy, for example, you might consider focusing your

Pyrography can be practiced on a specialized niche such as custom-made signs and presentation plaques. It will be entirely up to you to decide how intricate your pieces should be and whether or not to include a picture feature.

3. Find a way to link your work's theme to a personal interest. Are you, for example, a wildlife enthusiast? Consider the range of possibilities that this might open up for you. Not only could you use your theme to decorate your items but you could also use it to venture out into a new field where you could make more money.

For example, do you have a wildlife center nearby and if so, does it have a small shop or a café area?

Approach and ask them if they will be willing to exhibit and sell any of your wildlife products for you in exchange for a small percentage of sales but what else do you have to give them that could make the difference between being able to do this or being turned away?

4. The solution is to market yourself and your pyrography skills. You may offer to give a talk and a small demonstration about Pyrography, relating it to how you use sustainable woods and why you choose the theme of wildlife for your work. Perhaps you have an interest in environmental issues that you can integrate into your presentation and Pyrography demonstration.

Offer to take some raw wood samples to show near your job, along with a brief description of where you get your supplies and information about your Pyrography company and how people can contact you if they want to see more of your workplace a custom order.

If the wildlife center publicizes the case, they should profit from the increased public interest, resulting in increased sales in their shop/café and potential charitable donations. This would be excellent exposure for your Pyrography business and it could lead to new contacts and more innovative ideas.

CONCLUSION

Take a look at how past craftsmen and Pyrographers made and produced their work. They were true artisans, professional and dedicated craftspeople who put in a lot of time and effort into their work. They had the patience to persevere and had a high degree of competence due to their continued practice.

Perseverance is a quality that all Pyrographers must possess to achieve a high level of wood burning. Perseverance is more of a mental approach than a daunting task. You can be whoever or whatever you want! So, if you want to be the best at what you do, perseverance and willpower will get you there in the end!

Pyrographers in the past had a systematic approach to studying exacting methods for making various styles of work, such as portraits, landscapes and traditional designs.

Look through some old art books for ideas on pyrography, woodworking and other adaptable crafts. Old craft books can be found on eBay and Amazon and a search for antique and secondhand booksellers on the internet can yield a vast number of options to consider.

Old books on pyrography, arts and crafts and woodworking will teach you how to do things like inlay materials like wood or leather and create items using relief burning, which was once very common.

Books with old wood-burning drawings should be given special consideration. I'm not advising that you copy someone else's concept but looking through old drawings might help you develop new ideas for your work.

You may make your line of designs based on an old illustration and then redesign it with a brighter, more recent version of the same design. For example, you could come across an old photograph of three children skipping hand in hand.

You might modernize this by dressing them up in modern clothing and then burning the picture into a child's toy chest, for example. You must never explicitly copy anyone else's work unless the work is free of copyright; however, you can re-vamp and re-style it to make a new work of your own.

Many of the old books will teach you how to make Pyrography products. They go into how to use colors and how to use old polishing techniques to finish the job. You, too, can give your goods a real Wow factor by updating them with a fresh new image and paying attention to detail, just like the old craftsmen and Pyrographers did.

Arts and crafts can be used to communicate feelings that you may not convey verbally but if they can be released through creative expression, this may be a valuable way to restore harmony in your life.

Tapping into your spiritual subconscious' helps you explore and convey emotions from past and current thoughts by opening deeper areas of your subconscious mind. It's as if you're allowing yourself to enter a portal into your tale of past emotions.

If you've been through a tough emotional situation, such as divorce, the death of a loved one or illness, using art to heal some of the negative feelings that have been stuck within you might help you find a resolution and step forward towards a more hopeful future for yourself.

It can be difficult to take a step back from the chaos surrounding and impact us in our daily lives. Allowing ourselves time to reflect and access the deeper spiritual side of ourselves is important. This entails seeking a quiet location where we will not be disturbed.

Create a soothing and spiritual atmosphere for yourself, which you can accomplish by listening to soft natural or spiritual music. Make this 'your one-of-a-kind, all-about-you moment.' You must give the artist materials of your choice and, when ready, begin to release all negative emotional issues through colors, symbols, patterns and pictures.

The more you can do this in a healthy and peaceful atmosphere, and the less strong these negative emotions can become. Remember that you may feel drained and emotional when you first open up these wounds inside of you, so give yourself space and time to heal.

After tapping into your spiritual subconscious,' you may no longer need recovery and now experience a 'high,' as a new optimistic side of yourself takes over.

It is a stretch to say that you can release all of your negative emotions in one sitting! Allow yourself as many chances as possible to have "your special time," letting go of negative thoughts and allowing the positive light to shine through. The negativity will eventually fade away, allowing you to progress from strength to strength on your timetable.

WOODCARVING FOR BEGINNERS

The complete guide to make easy projects

By Antony Wood

© Copyright 2021 by Antony Wood

All rights reserved.

This document is geared towards providing exact and reliable information with regards to the topic and issue covered. The publication is sold with the idea that the publisher is not required to render accounting, officially permitted, or otherwise, qualified services. If advice is necessary, legal or professional, a practiced individual in the profession should be ordered.

From a Declaration of Principles which was accepted and approved equally by a Committee of the American Bar Association and a Committee of Publishers and Associations.

In no way is it legal to reproduce, duplicate, or transmit any part of this document in either electronic means or in printed format. Recording of this publication is strictly prohibited and any storage of this document is not allowed unless with written permission from the publisher. All rights reserved.

The information provided herein is stated to be truthful and consistent, in that any liability, in terms of inattention or otherwise, by any usage or abuse of any policies, processes, or directions contained within is the solitary and utter responsibility of the recipient reader. Under no circumstances will any legal responsibility or blame be held against the publisher for any reparation, damages, or monetary loss due to the information herein, either directly or indirectly.

Respective authors own all copyrights not held by the publisher.

The information herein is offered for informational purposes solely, and is universal as so. The presentation of the information is without contract or any type of guarantee assurance.

The trademarks that are used are without any consent, and the publication of the trademark is without permission or backing by the trademark owner. All trademarks and brands within this book are for clarifying purposes only and are the owned by the owners themselves, not affiliated with this document.

TABLE OF CONTENTS

INTRODUCTION..

CHAPTER 1..

What Is Wood Carving?..

CHAPTER 2..

Woodworking Tool Shapes, Sizes and Applications......

CHAPTER 3..

Wood Carving vs. Whittling...

CHAPTER 4..

Wood Carving - Understanding Wood Grain ....

CHAPTER 5..

How To Begin Wood Carving As A Hobby ....

CHAPTER 6..

What Tools Do You Need To Start Carving?..................

CHAPTER 7..

Wood Carved Projects For Beginners ....

How to Carve a Wooden Pipe ....

How To Carve Out A Dollhouse Out Of Wood ....

Carve a Dish with Basic Wood Carving.........................

Make a Knife for Wood carving.....................................

Carving Wooden Robots ....

CHAPTER 8 ....

Wood Carving - Cutting Angles and Bevels ....

CHAPTER 9 ....

Kickbacks on Table Saws for Wood Carving ....

CHAPTER 10 ....

Proper Proportions to Improve Your Wood Carving Caricatures ....

CHAPTER 11 ....

CHAPTER 12 ....

How to Sharpen Straight Chisels ....

CHAPTER 13 ....

How To Pick The Best Style Of Wood Carving ....

CHAPTER 14 ....

Choosing The Proper Woodcarving Knives And Taking Care Of Them ....

CHAPTER 15 ....

Protecting Your Wood Carving Knife Edges ....

CHAPTER 16 ....

Wood Carving Skill Make Money From Wood Carvings, Without You Carving Anything ....

CHAPTER 17 ....

Woodcarving Tips to Help You Along............................
CONCLUSION ....

INTRODUCTION

Nothing compares to creating something with your hands. Wood carving is a fantastic way to express yourself. From a piece of wood, you can make ornaments, figurines, decorations, toys, puzzles and sculptures, each with your unique vision of how the finished product should look.

Many people enjoy this hobby because it allows them to use their hands. The majority of woodcarvers work with only a piece of wood and a few hand tools. Hand-rubbed finishes improve the wood grain and detail of the piece.

The wood type you select will influence the amount of carving you can do. When you work with the wood grain, the piece becomes stronger. Working against the grain can make the piece more brittle.

Before determining where to begin carving, many woodworkers design their most intricate pieces.

Carving with the grain should be done on the thinnest or most delicate item.

Consider hardwoods that are durable when sanded to a fine grain for highly detailed or fine parts. Popular trees include maple, sycamore plum, pear, apple and Italian walnut. Choose the hardwood that is the most convenient for you to deal with all other tasks.

The most common woods are Tupelo, basswood, mahogany, chestnut, teak, and American walnut. Softwoods are less difficult to carve, but they don't last as long as hardwoods. A fuller grain is best for larger ventures and tight grain is better for detail work.

You can begin shaping your wood once you've chosen your wood and determined the best areas for your information. If the wood is hard and you have a lot of it to remove, you might want to start with a chisel and a mallet.

Start with a gouge and chip away layer after layer if it's not too difficult. On smaller projects, knives can

INTRODUCTION

Nothing compares to creating something with your hands. Wood carving is a fantastic way to express yourself. From a piece of wood, you can make ornaments, figurines, decorations, toys, puzzles and sculptures, each with your unique vision of how the finished product should look.

Many people enjoy this hobby because it allows them to use their hands. The majority of woodcarvers work with only a piece of wood and a few hand tools. Hand-rubbed finishes improve the wood grain and detail of the piece.

The wood type you select will influence the amount of carving you can do. When you work with the wood grain, the piece becomes stronger. Working against the grain can make the piece more brittle.

Before determining where to begin carving, many woodworkers design their most intricate pieces.

Carving with the grain should be done on the thinnest or most delicate item.

Consider hardwoods that are durable when sanded to a fine grain for highly detailed or fine parts. Popular trees include maple, sycamore plum, pear, apple and Italian walnut. Choose the hardwood that is the most convenient for you to deal with all other tasks.

The most common woods are Tupelo, basswood, mahogany, chestnut, teak, and American walnut. Softwoods are less difficult to carve, but they don't last as long as hardwoods. A fuller grain is best for larger ventures and tight grain is better for detail work.

You can begin shaping your wood once you've chosen your wood and determined the best areas for your information. If the wood is hard and you have a lot of it to remove, you might want to start with a chisel and a mallet.

Start with a gouge and chip away layer after layer if it's not too difficult. On smaller projects, knives can be used and on larger projects, saws and power tools can be used. Cutting or gouging against the grain is never a good idea. Always go for or against the grain.

Finishing tools come in a variety of shapes and sizes. What you use will be influenced by your creative vision of what the piece might look like. Chisels and gouges leave sharp lines that some people love. A rasp, which is a rough version of a file, can be used to smooth things out. Fine information can be smoothed out with smaller rasps and files.

A solid block of wood, a board, a dowel, a stump or an entire tree may all be used to carve. Dowels are easily carved for small projects, such as chess pieces. Dowel rods comes in variety of diameters and wood varieties. Some people can mix and match various types of wood to make one-of-a-kind pieces.

You will certainly enjoy the process of woodcarving, regardless of what you make. Are you ready to learn the basics to get started as a beginner.

Let's get started

CHAPTER 1

What Is Wood Carving?

Woodcarving is the art of using a tool to carve a figure, painting, pattern or sculpture into the wood. Woodcarving is an ancient craft that has been passed down over the years.

Wood carving is a technique for creating an image or motif on a wood item by creating a cavity in the object. As a consequence, the cavities come together to form an image or motif. The cavity is then referred to as relief.

This relief's motif contains unusual themes such as animals, plants and humans. Some themes also resemble the indentation style of the cosmos, beautiful embers or some other themes. A sculptor is solely responsible for deciding on this theme. Saws, planers, hammers and chisels are among the tools required to create a sculptural art piece.

The first sculpture was the product of Malayan culture or traditions. Art is believed to have existed for at least 500 years. It was also stated that Melaka, Kelantan and Negeri Sembilan had created a lot of this art to make traditional ornaments and decorations that were in the palace. Many people are familiar with wood carving art today. Wood carving artists have created various motives to raise public interest in wood carving.

Wood sculptures, modern and traditional musical instruments, furniture such as a bed a cupboard, chair, table and a headboat known as a stork, arms, cooking utensils, carpentry equipment and traditional transportation such as horse-drawn carriages, boats, ox-carts and so on can all be found at the gate today.

Wood carving art is currently flourishing in Indonesia's various regions. Jepara is one of Indonesia's most well-known regions for its wood carving craft. This area has created a wide range of wooden sculptures with a wide range of motives that rival Malayan works in beauty.

Rotary engraving means to engrave that is done with a rotating cutting tool in a motorized spindle. Rotary engraving can be done on some materials, but the most common in the awards industry are plastic, brass and aluminum.

In this case, a rotary engraving machine is required. Meanwhile, if you're looking for a suitable and inexpensive engraving machine for wood carving, a used engraving machine might be the solution.

Wood carving is a fun hobby that people of all ages can enjoy. A piece of wood can be transformed into practically anything and can be a wonderful way for the artist inside to express themselves. Beginners should start with the fundamentals of wood carving techniques and tools.

The first step for beginners in wood carving is to decide which technique they want to use. Whittling, relief carving, carving in the round and chip carving are the four major techniques. Cutting or extracting bits of wood from a piece of wood is known as whittling.

This is the basic form of wood carving, but it is becoming less common as modern wood carving focuses on complex and detailed designs. Relief carving is carving pictures into a flat piece of wood to create a three-dimensional portrait. This is often used to embellish signs or furniture.

As opposed to whittling, Carving in the round involves carving around the item, giving it a smooth and lifelike appearance. This method has the most versatility since any object can be transformed into a three-dimensional object.

Chip carving is the process of removing wood chips from a block of wood using knives or chisels to make patterns or designs. This method is often used to decorate household objects including chests. Each technique makes use of a unique collection of resources.

For beginners in wood carving, knowing what tools to use is important. Whittling is the simplest to learn because all you need is a sharp pocket knife and a wood block. It's also the cheapest and easiest way for a beginner to get started.

Chip carvers use only a few different knives to chip the wood surface and are a good way to get started in wood carving since they need fewer tools than other techniques.

Carving in the round necessitates using a greater range of materials, including knives, gouges and chisels. Almost any carving tool can be used in this technique, but different features can necessitate a different collection of tools.

Relief carving involves a simple carving kit to carve the images onto the wood, but the effect is primarily achieved with gouges. For beginners, carving in the round and relief carving can be difficult because they need more tools and patience.

For beginners, there are a variety of ways to get acquainted with wood carving. Experimenting with different tools and techniques is a perfect way for beginners to learn wood carving.

CHAPTER 2

Woodworking Tool Shapes, Sizes and Applications

Woodcarving can be a very beautiful craft. Whether for a hobby or decoration, woodcarvers worldwide enjoy carving different patterns and objects. The majority of woodcarvers do use basic tools.

Woodcarving is an art that hasn't changed much about how the artist goes about carving. A carving knife, a chisel, a gouge and a v tool, to name a few, are some of the most popular tools used by woodcarvers for their projects.

Many woodcarvers have multiples of each tool and they are crafted in a variety of shapes and sizes for various purposes. Some of the tools work on the piece complex, while others carve out more of the piece's outline.

There are many patterns to choose. Some are more informative for seasoned carvers, while others are for beginners. Birds, dragons, trees, landscapes, humans, deer, bears and other animals are among the most common patterns.

Depending on your creative ability, you might be able to do a free-form carving based on an image or improvise the carving without using a picture. On the other hand, majority of people choose to buy or look for informative trends. This guide will walk you through the majority of the information you'll need to start carving as a beginner.

Another decision you'll have to make while carving is what kind of wood you'll use. Carvers refer to them as either hardwood or softwood. Oak, rosewood, sandalwood and walnut are examples of hardwood. Oak, cedar and fir are some examples of softwood. Softwood is much simpler to deal with than hardwood. Softwood does not splinter or cut as easily as hardwood.

Woodcarving can often become more than just a pastime. Some people exhibit their work at festivals and fairs and sell it to the general public. Some advertise that for a fee, and can carve an image of your choice in wood. Others create their schools or workshops to help others learn about the craft. However, whether you are carving for pleasure or profit, you must share your passion for helping keep the art alive.

Chainsaw carving is similar to woodcarving in that the main tool is a chainsaw and the result is usually a life-size version of the pattern desired. Chainsaw carving is becoming increasingly popular around the world. At shows and expos, there is a type of speed carving usually well-received by attendees.

Having the ability to carve intricate designs out of imported timbers, furniture timbers and cabinet timbers and use them as furniture in your home will save you a lot of money and give your home a unique touch. You can make beds, tables and chairs, among other items.

If you want to pursue woodcarving as a hobby or start a business carving imported wood, furniture timber or cabinet timbers into works of art, you'll need the following materials. Except for parting tools, measuring a woodworking tool requires measuring the tool's cutting point's widest portion. A tool's name often defines its intent.

Parting Tools - They have a V-shaped cutting edge that is usually .45" or .60" long. It can be used on furniture woods, imported timbers and cabinet woods for roughing out or finishing inside corners.

Veining Equipment - has a deep U-shaped cutting edge for grooving and roughing out small areas and can be used on furniture, imported woods and cabinet wood.

Fluters, also called firmers, are straight gouges larger and wider than veining tools and can be used on furniture, imported and cabinet woods.

Chisels - can be used for flat-cutting and finishing of furniture, imported and cabinet woods.

Skews are a form of the chisel with a straight cutting edge that's great for cornering and can be used on furniture, imported woods and cabinet woods.

Long-Bent Gouges - also known as a curved fluter, this tool performs similar functions and can be used on furniture, imported woods and cabinet woods.

The Spoon Gouge, also known as a short-bent gouge, has a straight shank and a spoon-shaped bend on the cutting edge. It can be used on furniture woods, imported timbers and cabinet woods to smooth out surfaces.

Back-Bent Gouges - similar to spoon gouges, but with a convex-shaped curve that bends backward. They're great for clearing undersides and work well with furniture, imported woods and cabinet wood.

Fish Tail Gouges - allow for clean cuts in close quarters or corners and be used as a straight gouge. They can be used with furniture woods, imported timbers and cabinet woods.

Amateur tools are recommended for those who are just getting started. These tools usually have shorter shanks than professional tools, which makes them easier to handle. After you've honed your skills with amateur equipment, upgrade to skilled grade tools.

CHAPTER 3

Wood Carving vs. Whittling

The cutting of small bits from a woodpiece or removal of pare shavings is known as whittling. It is the simplest type of wood carving, but it is not the wood carving art as we know it today.

Wood carving necessitates a range of tools, including power tools. As a result, things could quickly become complicated. When one whittles, though, this is not the case. To whittle, you just need two things: a piece of wood and a knife.

True whittling has always been a straightforward operation. The wood's details aren't particularly refined but rather rough. You can tell when you're holding a whittled object in your lap.

Each knife stroke is noticeable. It's not possible to use sandpaper. This is the polar opposite of wood carving, which is known for its meticulous attention to detail. You normally won't see a single knife stroke while holding a wood carving of the same thing.

It's a fascinating subject. When all you have is a knife, whittling a little girl could take a week. It takes more tools to carve the same little girl out of wood, but it takes a fraction of the time. She'll also have a lot of information that would be impossible to do with only a knife.

Whittling does not necessitate any special equipment, circumstances or working environment. It just takes you, a piece of wood and your knife. Whittle can be done inside or outside the house, in a car, at a picnic, in a park or about anywhere. This isn't the case for intricate wood carving.

When you carve wood, you'll almost certainly need a range of specialized tools. Info knives and carving knives, wood rasps and files, wood gouges and wood chisels are all available. Those aren't the only ones. (Do you know what a sanding stick is?) There's a fair chance you'll have a few power tools in your wood carving toolbox. Then you'll have to think about how you're going to get electricity. It's not that easy.

When it comes to wood carving, you do need a dedicated workspace. Much of the time, you're not even keeping the wood you're dealing with. A vise will always do the job for you, so you'll need a strong workbench or platform and you don't want someone messing with those priceless tools. Aside from the chance of losing them, all of them are incredibly sharp and can only be treated by you.

What about the unique development you've been working on for such a long time?

You don't want any onlookers scoping it out while you're not there. Who knows what will occur.

What happened to the nose?

Whittling is thought to be a contemplative and meditative practice. It's not so much about what you're whittling as it is about the process. Wood carving is more of a finished product. You aspire to build what you see in your head, complete with all the details. You cannot have time to spare because you have a product to make.

It boils down to personal preference. Whittling is for you if you don't care about rushing and want to take your time to see what happens. Wood carving could be just what you're looking for if you want to see how talented you are and how good you are at bringing out info.

CHAPTER 4

Wood Carving - Understanding Wood Grain

There are lots of things to learn about wood carving for beginners and not understanding wood grain is a source of frustration and disappointment. Cutting in the wrong direction for the wood grain will result in disintegration, division or damage in the grain. To summarize, wood carving without consideration for the grain direction can result in unfavorable wooden chunks.

When you probe a piece of wood, you will note that it is made up of what seems to be a cluster of tubes jammed together shoulder to shoulder. Imagine a bunch of pipes glued together shoulder to shoulder and that's how the wood grain looks.

The tree's vascular bundle portion is responsible for assisting in the transfer of minerals within the tree.

Beginners in wood carving should pay attention to the tubes' direction because it is crucial in determining which path to carve. For beginners, there are two types of cuts to consider: cutting with the grain or cutting against the grain.

When making any cuts, cut with the grain so that the knife can pass through the wood without being wedged between the fibers. Carving with the grain can be frustrating because the cut's direction varies depending on the pieces you're holding and removing.

When cutting with the grain, there are two things to remember for beginners: which course the tubes are lengthwise and which section of the cut you are holding and which side you are eradicating. You can need to cut at a 90-degree angle or a sideways angle to the vascular bundle tubes on occasion.

You can cut from left to right or right to left and depending on the side of the cut you're conserving, either one can be the way that goes with the grain. The general rule is to carve away from the hand you're preserving. If you're making a cut and want to save the segment to the left of the cut, for example, you'll cut from left to right and vice versa.

You'll need to carve into the ends of the grains in certain cases. A gouge or v-tool would work well for cutting. However, if you want to cut with a knife, you'll need to plan out the cut course ahead of time. This is a delicate technique since you must cut in the direction of the grain's end. To get the cut you want, you'll have to make some small cuts.

Cutting with the grain seems to be an easy task, but what if you can't see the grain?

This wood carving project for beginners may appear intimidating at first. As a result, it's best to avoid cutting into the wood with wild grain patterns; however, you'll have to make small shallow cuts to decide the grain's direction if you must. When cutting with the grain, the cuts are smooth and painless; when carving against the grain, the cuts are more difficult.

Wood carving or the art of cutting designs into wood has been practiced since the dawn of time. Knives, saws and gouges, among other common tools, have been used to achieve various techniques. Floral designs, geometrical patterns and abstract design decorative panels have all been made.

Furniture, spoons, plates, toys, trays, jewel boxes, vases, book stands, masks, icons, frames, beads, chess sets and whatever else the imagination might conjure up have all been made from it. Wood carving has been passed down from one generation to another since the beginning.

Anyone can carve hand tools, eating utensils, figurines and much more with only a few tools and a variety of almost any kind of used wood. Carving ability and repertoire can develop as a person's carving expertise increases. An individual could eventually be regarded as a master woodcarver.

A good woodcarver uses a good collection of carving tools, but it's also important to use good wood carving. When starting with this project, softwoods are recommended. Gymnosperm trees are known as softwoods. Except for bald cypress trees, they are mostly evergreen trees. Softwood accounts for 80% of all global timber supply.

The Linden tree is a great wood for carving. It's a soft, easy-to-work-with wood. It has a low density and little grain. For the Vikings, it was abundant and simple to obtain. It was common among them for carving shields and other objects. Carving intricate designs in linden wood was easy. This wood was used in many sculptures and intricate altarpieces throughout the Middle Ages.

It's also a fine wood for producing high-quality guitars and wind instruments. It's also powerful enough to be used for drum shells, both in sound and aesthetics. This wood is also famous for window shutters and blinds.

Hardwood is the polar opposite of softwood. Angiosperm is the name for this type of tree. Softwood, contrary to common opinion, is not always softer than hardwood. Since the density of wood hardness varies, some hardwoods are harder than most softwoods.

Some hardwoods are found to be much tougher than longleaf pines, Douglas fir and yew. Working with chestnut, butternut, oak, American walnut, mahogany and teak is also a good idea.

The olive tree is an outstanding hardwood for carving. Olive trees' gnarled, twisted trunks produce elegant, aromatic wood used to make bowls, knife handles and furniture inlays. Olive wood often burns hot, produces little smoke, is aromatic and is ideal for cooking. It's great for baking bread on breadboards, grilling foods and smoking meats.

Olive wood is thick, hard and long-lasting. It has a distinctive hue, with reds, grays and browns in various shades. It is durable and long-lasting. For centuries, it has piqued the interest of woodcarvers. Once someone has mastered softwood carving, they may want to try their hand at this lovely wood.

CHAPTER 5

How To Begin Wood Carving As A Hobby

Woodcarving is a type of art and language and it is possibly the oldest woodworking skill. According to what I've learned, it appears to have arisen in the Middle Ages in Italy and France and then spread throughout the world. It's extremely satisfying to take a block of wood and turn it into something special and expressive.

Learning how to carve wood is a difficult skill to master. Wood carving has become increasingly popular among hobbyists and people have realized that it is a simple art that requires both skill and imagination.

It's time to move on to more intricate projects once you've mastered the fundamentals of wood carving. However, as previously mentioned, you must first learn the fundamentals and practice wood carving as a beginner. You'll be able to move on to producing your masterpieces after that.

A step-by-step tutorial on how to carve wood can be found here. After reading the instructions, you should be able to begin your wood carving project.

Step 1: Gather the required materials. You will, of course, need wood to carve it. There are many different types of wood to choose from. Woods come in a variety of shapes, sizes and types. It is advisable for beginners to start with a softwood variety. While hardwood is suitable for wood carving, it would be difficult for a beginner to master.

Step 2: Settle on a concept. Wood can be used to carve some items. One thing to keep in mind is that you should select a wood size that will suit the design you want to carve.

Step 3: Draw a rough plan sketch. After you've found the right template, you'll need to trace it onto your piece of wood. Any kind of marker will suffice as long as it can lead you in the right direction by leaving visible marks on the area you need to carve out.

Step 4: Begin chopping. For this, you'll need to find the necessary equipment. On the other hand, finer details would necessitate the use of specialized tools that would allow you to carve through even the tiniest of details.

Step 5: Complete your masterpiece by smoothing it out. There will always be rough edges in your wood carving, no matter how hard you practice or how skilled you become. You'll need smoothing tools like sandpaper for these. Scrub away the rough edges until you see the flawless outline you dreamed of in your design.

Step 6: Complete the task. A piece of wood with a smooth finish is often appealing. Since color can detract from your work's beauty, it is not recommended that you use paint. To improve your wood product's appearance, you may use walnut oil, natural stains, or varnish.

Choose Your Medium

If your woodcarving abilities have advanced beyond whittling on the front porch in your spare time, now is the time to research the various media that can help you take your skills to the next stage.

There are many options out there waiting for art lovers like you to discover the artist inside, allowing you to create simple or complex works of art that can become family heirlooms, earn you some extra cash or simply provide you with tremendous personal satisfaction. Here's a short rundown of the various types of materials that make woodworking so enjoyable for millions of people like you.

Sugar Pine: Also known as sugar pine, this type of wood is a white variety that grows primarily in the western United States and is one of the largest known species. It's one of the most common wood carving mediums and it's typically used to carve small animals or other figures.

Jelutong: Despite being technically hardwood, jelutong is valued in the woodworking world for its fine texture and straight grain. These characteristics make jelutong simple to work with, making it an excellent choice for both beginners and experts.

Tupelo: Not only is Tupelo coveted by woodcarvers, but it also has the distinction of being the name of a settlement! It's white and smooth, with a grain that comes to life when stained.

If you enjoy power carving, this is a great option for you; however, hand carvers will appreciate its ease of use with wood carving tools. Since it comes from swampy places, choose parts free of rot and discoloration and come from the tree's bottom bell.

Ash Wood: If you want to make walking sticks, look for hardwoods like ash. Brittle woods just won't do if you want to use your walking sticks. Ash has the best mix of toughness and versatility with just the right amount of elasticity. Ash is a light-colored wood that stains beautifully, as its name suggests.

The style and techniques used differ from person to person, as they do with so many other art types. There are a few fundamentals to learning woodcarving that relate to the majority of people.

Be gentle with yourself and start small when choosing the first few projects. If you want to push a project too far, you will become frustrated and abandon something you genuinely enjoy.

Purchase a simple collection of carving tools of decent quality. A chisel, bent gouge bent chisel, skew, straight gouge and bent v-parting tool are generally included in a simple beginner kit. It's all too tempting to get carried away with your tool purchases.

I discovered a website with over 20,000 different woodworking tools. You don't have to start with the most expensive tools, but you can make sure they're of high quality. When you get more involved with your art, you will increase the number of tools you have and eventually increasing your tool collection is less costly.

Pick up a book or two that appeals to your passion and will teach you how to carve. I would also recommend searching for a carving club or even just a group of people to carve within your city. It's hard make jelutong simple to work with, making it an excellent choice for both beginners and experts.

Tupelo: Not only is Tupelo coveted by woodcarvers, but it also has the distinction of being the name of a settlement! It's white and smooth, with a grain that comes to life when stained.

If you enjoy power carving, this is a great option for you; however, hand carvers will appreciate its ease of use with wood carving tools. Since it comes from swampy places, choose parts free of rot and discoloration and come from the tree's bottom bell.

Ash Wood: If you want to make walking sticks, look for hardwoods like ash. Brittle woods just won't do if you want to use your walking sticks. Ash has the best mix of toughness and versatility with just the right amount of elasticity. Ash is a light-colored wood that stains beautifully, as its name suggests.

The style and techniques used differ from person to person, as they do with so many other art types. There are a few fundamentals to learning woodcarving that relate to the majority of people.

Be gentle with yourself and start small when choosing the first few projects. If you want to push a project too far, you will become frustrated and abandon something you genuinely enjoy.

Purchase a simple collection of carving tools of decent quality. A chisel, bent gouge bent chisel, skew, straight gouge and bent v-parting tool are generally included in a simple beginner kit. It's all too tempting to get carried away with your tool purchases.

I discovered a website with over 20,000 different woodworking tools. You don't have to start with the most expensive tools, but you can make sure they're of high quality. When you get more involved with your art, you will increase the number of tools you have and eventually increasing your tool collection is less costly.

Pick up a book or two that appeals to your passion and will teach you how to carve. I would also recommend searching for a carving club or even just a group of people to carve within your city. It's hard to overestimate the importance of watching and listening to others in your profession.

Find out if any classes are being offered in your city or if a woodworking store offers any demonstrations. Don't give up if you can't find any classes or assistance in your field. There are videos on the internet that can help and I know some self-taught carvers who create beautiful work.

Among the most important things you'll need to get started is a piece of wood. If you're making a hand-held piece, softwoods like butternut, aspen or basswood are excellent choices. For the first few projects, any of those three will be ideal.

Since softwoods like basswood don't take stains well, many people opt to paint their finished product. Harder woods, such as walnut, mahogany and cherry, have a beautiful grain pattern that can be enhanced with a light stain, but they are more difficult to carve due to the grain.

If you're starting with rough woods, you'll need a mallet in your toolkit. Once you've decided on the wood, draw out the design with a pencil, pass the design to the wood with granite paper and you're ready to go.

Always think about safety first! When carving, don't keep your wood in your lap; instead, secure it to a table or use a vice to hold it. You'll be using force to drive the knife or gouge into the wood all of the time and it'll slip a lot.

If you're going to carry the item you're carving, I'd suggest having a proper glove for the hand you'll use to hold the wood before you begin. Highly cut-resistant gloves are available. This isn't to say that you shouldn't poke your hand and that you shouldn't use serrated blades or cutting instruments with caution, but it will help you save money on band-aids.

When carving, wear protective goggles to prevent a tiny chip of wood from flying into your eye. When you're ready for power tools, make sure to add a dust mask to your list of protection products so you don't inhale dust all the time.

Woodcarving is not an easy art to master; it is typically done in stages, but it is one of the most enjoyable hobbies or pastimes, in my view. It can be one of the easiest woodworking projects to begin with, but it can also be a wonderful way to express yourself and a lot of fun.

CHAPTER 6

What Tools Do You Need To Start Carving?

Answering the question, "What "tools" do you need to carve anything out of wood?" will take some thought and practice. The list that follows is an unusual list of the carving "tools" you'll need to get started carving as a hobby or a side business.

1: The ability to see, that is, to note all of the specifics of the bird or animal you want to carve.

2: The ability to do the requisite research to learn as much as possible about the object you intend to carve, such as its habitat.

3: The perseverance to see the carving project through until it is completed to your satisfaction.

4: Your real hand-held equipment can include any or more of the following: a couple of books on "carving" Knives and chisels for wood carving—an electric rotary carving tool (Dremel or Foredom) with a large selection of carving pieces.

A hole-drilling tool and a small electric band saw (table mounted electric drill press or small electric hand drill). Acrylic paints and paintbrushes are included. To clear carving dust, use a shop vacuum.

I began carving with a knife a few years ago and eventually progressed from carving all by hand to the much faster and better method of carving known as electric rotary carving.

I purchased a couple of wood carving magazines to help me develop my skills as a woodcarver. Those magazines were a valuable resource because their articles taught me how to carve and what to carve. They also provided a wealth of information on designs, raw wood, carving books and other tools needed for good carving.

The more carving you do, the stronger your carvings will become because each new carving project will provide you with a new set of challenges to overcome. You may have to learn to work around an unseen knot or blemish in the wood. You must consider where the bird's eyes and feet should be placed for them to appear balanced and normal.

Since most finished carvings are shown on a stand or pedestal, you'll need to learn how to create various mounting options. Once you've completed the actual woodcarving, you'll need to learn how to use acrylic paints to make your carving as appealing as possible.

Before you pick up a carving knife or one of the electric rotary carving tools, read as many books and magazine articles as you can about wood carving. Then start with something quick and easy to carve and work your way up to more complex projects.

Wood carving necessitates study, consideration, preparation and a great deal of patience to produce a carving that you would be proud to display on a shelf and say: "I entirely carved that! Is it possible for me to show you how to carve?"

You'll need a variety of resources if you want to be a woodcarver rather than just a whittler. There's no getting around it.

So, what are the best wood carving tools?

Sharpening utensils Tools for sharpening carving tools should probably come first, before the carving tools. After all, what good are they if they aren't sharp? You're going to make yourself insane.

You should have a strop and a sharpening stone at the very least. The sharpening stone is used to ensure that your edges are razor-sharp. Sharpening stones are available in a variety of shapes and sizes.

Some are very tolerant of the wood carving blade edges' normally short blade lengths. Sharpening an edge with diamond-coated slip stones is very effective. Some sharpening stones are small enough to fit on a key chain or a credit card. It's so easy.

A strop is used to extract the burr and any remaining micro-bits from your sharpened blade tip. In wood carving, this is important. If something is clinging to the edge, it'll hinder your advancement. You've got to get rid of everything. If you prefer, you can smooth out the edges with a honing compound or a honing surface.

Shaping Instruments

Each type of carving tool used to form wood has a distinct purpose. You should have carving knives, wood gouges, wood chisels wood rifflers and rasps, a mallet and probably a power drill at the very least.

Carving knives - This is the most fundamental of all carving instruments and there are many different types. Straight-edged knives, bent knives, detail knives, twisted knives chip knives, special pocket knives modified for folding and carving knives with lockable blades are among the various types knives available. Those aren't the only ones. If you like, you can also get micro-knives or micro-tool kits.

It's all about features. Every edge has a distinct goal. You'll know which knives are best for the job after you've studied what each form of the knife can do and considered the carving project at hand. The best knives for one mission may not be the same as the best knives for another. That is why you have options.

Chisels made of wood - While most chisels are ground on both sides, it is possible to find ones with only one side bevel. The form of the head may be slanted or square. They may also be bending forward or backward. You'll have a lot of options.

Wood Gouges - This is one of the most commonly used carving materials. There are a variety of shapes and sizes available. Others are very short and stout, while others have an extended blade edge that extends for a few inches. You'll almost definitely end up with some them. That isn't a problem. You'll almost certainly need each one at some stage.

Riffler files or wood rasps - Shopping for these tools would likely be perplexing. It's true. Some stores refer to it as a rasp, whereas others refer to it as a riffler. Another will refer to it as a rasp riffler.

A rasp, according to the majority of merchants, is a very coarse, straight paper. The tool may look like a sharpening file and be thick and rectangular, but don't be surprised if it's slender with a curving head and looks like a riffler.

Rifflers, on the other hand, have a curved head and are normally slender. These curved heads are commonly found on both ends of the riffler. You will also find kits that include some different shaped and sized heads.

Mallets are a form of the mallet. In the right situation, these small hammers can be extremely useful. Chip carving, relief carving and intaglio carving all include them.

(What am I trying to say?)

Wood carving includes the use of mallets. You would just need a few millimeters off here and there and maybe a notch here, an indent there and a shadow there. It's an extremely useful tool.

Powerful tools - Wood carving power tools are available in some designs. Power drills, power chisels, rotor saw burrs and mini grinders are all available. Power carving kits are also available.

There's even a package for woodcarvers that comes with its set of power grinders.

The amount of time and labor these tools can save woodcarvers is astounding. Many people think of them as only being suitable for life-size or incredibly large carvings. All is up to the carver. How about a carving completely made of power tools? (I'm not sure how high that will be.)

Sanding and smoothing tools. After you've finished carving and shaping the wood, sand and smooth all of the surfaces, this is a crucial step that must be completed before any painting or varnishing can begin.

You need to prepare the wood to bond with non-penetrating chemicals by removing any residue from any previous finishing procedure. Sandpaper, sanding sticks or sanding clothes may all be used for sanding.

Sanding is mostly done with sandpaper. There are many different grades, ranging from very coarse to very fine. There's a lot to choose from. The de-fuzzing pad is a product that is very similar to this. It does just as it says on the tin. It gets rid of any residual fuzz on the wood's surface.

Sanding clothes come in rolls and are available in a variety of grit sizes. Parts of the roll can be cut and rolled or folded as desired. The good part is that you won't have to think about it breaking or crumbling under your feet.

Sanding sticks are also available in a variety of grit sizes. You may also get sanding stick kits or sanding detail kits to get rid of glue and other small remnants of your finished items. For large sanding work, sanding belts or mini-belt sanding sticks can be used.

Wood carving is a great ability to master. You could deal with small projects with just a few materials. You may also work on massive projects using a variety of tools, including power tools. In any case, it's incredibly calming, exhilarating and fulfilling.

CHAPTER 7

Wood Carved Projects For Beginners

Wood carving is a perfect way to make simple wood look more interesting. Wood carving is a skill that can be done as a hobby or as part-time work. Woodcarving allows a person to express his or her imagination while also adding decor to the living room.

You may be interested in learning how to carve wood. You can form the wood in a few different ways. Before we get into that, let's look at why wood is used in the first place.

People who care about the environment tend to use wood because it reduces carbon emissions by nearly ten to twenty percent. Since timber is the only commodity that comes from a sustainable resource, it quickly becomes the material of choice for most people. Let's look at the different ways to carve wood by examining the steps outlined below.

Get a piece of wood. Choose softwoods such as butternut, basswood and others if you are a beginner.

Collect a collection of carving tools. Chisel the wood with a utility knife. Make sure your methods are razor-sharp.

Build a design now. Use graphite paper, create a hand-drawn template. You might only draw directly on the wood. Make the design clear, as this will allow you to learn more while working on it.

With a small knife, begin carving. An x-acto knife is suitable for beginners. Later on, you can start with a utility knife and work your way up to a more advanced carving knife.

To cut out designs with ease, go with the grain. Pound the chisel's apex with a sledgehammer. Make sure you're turning the chisel in the same direction as the pattern patterns. When carving, it's a good idea to wear goggles and gloves.

Clear the debris out of the way so you can study the carvings. Later on, you can add more info. Use stain to cover your finished piece is a good idea.

How to Carve a Wooden Pipe

Knowing how to carve wood is incredibly useful because it helps you to make appealing and beautiful artwork. This ability can also be used to make one-of-a-kind and trendy items that you can sell to others.

A wooden pipe is one thing you can make if you know how to carve wood. It is best to follow the simple steps for making a wooden pipe if you want to earn extra money.

Artists are encouraged to collect and plan all of the materials required for this activity before beginning the project. Bruyere wood is the most important component of the project.

If you can't find Bruyere wood, you can use some kind of wood or a briar block in its place. You'll also need carving materials and equipment including a milling cutter, a chisel, a grafter, sandpaper, a saw, a Dremel tool, a drill and a pencil, also to the wood.

After you've prepared the equipment and supplies, you'll need to decide on a pipe pattern. You can get ideas for various pipe designs by surfing the Internet or looking through magazines and books. If you got the template from a website, you could print it to refer to it whenever you forget the information.

Visualize how the finished product will look. Use the pencil, draw a rough outline of the design on the wood. Take out the saw and cut or remove the excess wood with it. If you don't want to have any issues, make sure you cut the wood according to the outline.

Make a loop at the pipe's widest point. In the first circle, draw another circle. These diagrams are vital since they will guide the creation of the hollow portion of the pipe.

Draw the mouthpiece into the wood's narrowest section. Get the drill and cut the holes in the wooden pipe with it. To make it more fun and tempting, make sure you know the pipe's exact dimensions before drilling. Take out the chisel and use it to finish the pipe's interior.

After that, use the saw to hack away any excess wood. Finish the exposed or exterior portion of the finished product with sandpaper. To improve its appearance, apply a coat of lacquer or sealant.

How To Carve Out A Dollhouse Out Of Wood

Your daughter is in the market for a new dollhouse. You are a professional woodcarver. This is the ideal time to put your hobby to good use and create something that both you and she will be proud of.

A blueprint for constructing a wooden dollhouse can be found here. It could be a lovely dollhouse for playtime with fashion dolls if hanging low on a wall in her home. Alternatively, instead of hanging it on the wall, it can be put on top of her dresser.

Components

- 3 pieces 36" long for horizontal shelves and two 33" long pieces for vertical sides of 1' wide x 1" thick boards

- One 34-inch-long, 12-inch-thick, 2-inch-wide board for hanging her dollhouse on the wall

- Twelve 2" long wood screws for attaching vertical boards to the shelving

- For attaching the narrow support board underneath the topmost horizontal board, use four wood screws at least 2" long.

- Spackle to cover the screw holes with wood putty

- Three long bolts for hanging heavier shelves on drywall or plasterboard

- A paintbrush and one pint of clear acrylic varnish

• sandpaper (fine)

Instruments

• Drill with a battery or an electric motor

• A level for leveling the dollhouse

• Marking down holes for drilling with a pencil and tape measure

Methodology

1) Before assembly, varnish and sand the wood lengths with three acrylic varnish coats, sanding in between coats. Just use a soft contact for the final sanding. To make cleanup simpler, use transparent acrylic varnish.

2) Lay out the doll house's assembly. The horizontal bits or shelves, will be the three 36" longboards. The sides will be 33" longboards.

3) Screw the narrower board for hanging her dollhouse underneath the upper horizontal board on the wall-facing side. In four positions, screw in the 2" screws.

4) Connect the upper assembly to both ends of vertical boards from the exterior to the interior with two 2" screws on both ends. Your top is now full.

5) If you have 18" dolls, space the centerboard so that one of the openings is at least 19" high. Just like the upper board, screw it into the sides.

6) At both ends, screw two of the 2" screws into the bottom horizontal board.

Completing

- For a professional, good finish, screws should be recessed and filled in with wood putty.

- Enlist a friend's assistance to hang your assembly on the wall using the three bolts given.

Finally, take a step back and enjoy your work before presenting the dolls with their new home! When not in use, store inside a large cedar unfinished chest to keep it intact.

Carve a Dish with Basic Wood Carving

Choose a basic form, such as a leaf, to begin with. Examine some trees and choose a leaf shape that appeal to you. Choose a wood block with a firm, near grain, such as chestnut, mahogany or walnut and later maple and ash.

Draw the concept first on paper since it's much easier to alter or adjust a drawing than to modify wood after being cut. The carpenter's motto is to think twice before making a single cut.

After tracing your pattern onto the wood and running it diagonally or parallel to the grain, use a fret saw to cut out the shape of your leaf close to the outline. It can now be glued to a bigger, lower-quality piece of wood than the work that can be reused for this purpose, which is to tie it down to the bench.

A sheet of newspaper was placed between the two glued parts to allow the work to be separated after the face was carved, making it easier to remove them after completion.

The suggested gouge is No 6 or 7 and begins shaping the inside from the grain's direction, which is the simplest method; sadly, carving into wood is easier than carving out of wood. The wood fibers are compressed when cut when cutting into it, but they are opened up and ripped apart when cutting out.

It's like trying to sharpen a pencil with a penknife by starting at the point and cutting back toward yourself rather than cutting towards the point, which is much quicker and safer.

Instead of carving from the closest hand, take a tiny chip from the farthest side of the work away from yourself and proceed until you've removed all you want. Finish by sandpapering the surface and mixing it in.

Make a Knife for Wood carving

I decided to try making carving knives after seeing a few articles and tutorials on the subject. The majority of the instructional material I've found explains how to make your knife, from the blade to the handle.

I don't have any of the necessary equipment or skills to make my blades, so when I came across some ideas for using an old pocket knife blade, I jumped at the chance to give it a shot. I decided to share the details with my guests because it turned out well.

The first move is to locate the old knife from which you want to extract a blade. After extracting the blade from the pocket knife, cut out a 3/4" by 3/4" by 5" piece of desired wood for the handle (I'm using hickory) and break it in half.

Now draw a line across the part of the blade that will be recessed within the handle and cut a notch out of it so that the blade is flush with that half of the handle. Drill a hole through both halves where the blade will be held in place with a screw and then drill another hole through both halves closer to the other end of the handle with a drill. For the pins in this project, I used a couple of nails.

Now that you've done a dry run of placing the two halves together with the nails and blade in place, it's time to add JB Weld or 5 Minute Epoxy within the blade recess and quickly place the blade in.

More bonding compounds can now be applied to the other side of the blade recess and the two halves of wood. Attach the two halves with the nails. Clamp the knife with a clamp to ensure a tightened fit for drying. Any of the excess bonding material that squeezes out may need to be wiped away.

Remove the clamps after allowing the clamped knife to dry for 24 hours. Cut the nails flush with the wooden handle with a cutoff wheel or hacksaw, and then sand the knife smooth with a sander. To round off the corners and smooth out the cut-off nails, I used a power hand sander.

You've now produced a carving knife that you will be proud of. You can use a wood burner to burn your initials into the handle or carve a pattern into the handle with another knife.

You can now either leave the handle natural or seal it with your preferred finish. Remember to sharpen your new carving knife using your chosen method to ensure it is razor-sharp and ready to use.

Carving Wooden Robots

Since the early 1990s, I've been wood carving robots as a hobby. I've had a lot of fun carving these little robots. You may want to put some time into this art and I can assure you that you will not be disappointed.

To begin, you'll need a lot of patience and a strong desire to build or carve wood robots. I have a good reason for this. I've loved collecting space figures, space robots and all things space since I was a child. In reality, I wanted to be an astronaut at one point, but it didn't work out. As a result, I'm trying to persuade others to appreciate the art of wood carving robots.

After that, you'll need to buy a decent carving knife, which you can get from a good hobby store or a wood carving supply house. The best advice is to keep the blade at an inch or an inch and a half thick.

There's a reason for this: you can perform faster with a short blade than you can with a long one and you'll avoid injuries. That's right, the risk of cutting your fingers exists and the more precautions you take, the better. Don't let this bother you; if you're cautious, you'll have few injuries.

Let me continue talking about carving knives. It is my suggestion that you choose a tool that feels good on your side. The handle of the knife should be much wider than the blade. The explanation for this is to give you more power when carving your wood robot.

By the way, don't expect the robot to shift until you've completed your project—only a little sarcasm on my part. Let me begin by saying that a decent carving knife nowadays costs about $20 or more.

What qualities do you want in a fine carving knife?

Any good carver will tell you the same thing I do: it needs to be razor-sharp! Yes, the knife must be made of the highest-quality steel and have a razor-sharp tip. If you take nothing else from this chapter, remember that wood carving robots requires patience and a razor-sharp knife.

Carving Chisels and Woods

Wood carving, also known as Xyloglyphy, is the method of carving a figure from a wood block using the necessary tools. To summarize, the wood's consistency, the accuracy of the tools and the artist's experience combine to create some of the most beautiful wood figures we have ever seen. From the Middle Ages, say 500 to 1500 BCE, Christian iconography influenced early wood carvings in Italy and France.

Wood carving originated in Japan around the same time as the figures of Christ, in Buddhist sculptures. 6000-year-old wood carvings of a male figure made of black sycamore and inlaid with bronze ebony and crystals have been discovered in Ancient Egypt.

Range of Wood

The consistency of the finished product is primarily determined by the wood used. Wood is anisotropic, meaning it does not have the same consistency around as metal. The 'grain' reflects the direction in which the wood would be strongest and it is recommended that all delicate work in wood be done along the grain rather than against it.

The grain reflects texture variations such as wavy interlocked or strait. The fact that carving along the grain is better shows that tender, cross-grain designs break quickly, while those done along the grain last longer.

Hardwoods such as Basswood and Tupelo and chestnut, maple, Mahogany, Teak and Rosewood, are considered excellent wood carvings. Italian walnut, maple, apple and pear carving is renowned for their delicacy.

The instruments

Whittling is the basic form of wood carving and is mostly used on softwoods. It is primarily done as a hobby and the quality and beauty of the products created by these amateurs will astound you. Knives are the only tools used in this craft; no chisels or other tools are used.

A workbench and gadget to keep the wood to the workbench are the most basic wood carving requirements. The carving knife is used to pare, cut and smooth the wood surface; the gouge, with curved cutting edges, aids in the formation of hollows, rounds and curves; the chopping saw is used to cut the wood chunks as a whole; the chisel, a straight-edged blade used in leveling; the v-tool is used for parting; the veneer is a special gouge with a u-shaped cutting edge; a wooden mallet and

The work of art

The wood type used to carve the sculpture is extremely significant. It's important to note that hardwoods are difficult to carve but last a long time, while softwoods are easy to deal with but don't last as long and are more likely to be destroyed. Intricate designs, on the other hand, will necessitate fine-grained wood.

After the wood selection process is finished, the gouging and shaping of the wood will begin in earnest. It's important to make sure that the tools you're using are consistent with the hard or softwood you're working with.

The sculptor now uses the chisel, gouge and v-tool to refine the basic form, with the mallet for finer details if appropriate. After the work is completed, a protective layer of wax or lacquer is added.

CHAPTER 8

Wood Carving - Cutting Angles and Bevels

Cutting instruments make up the majority of wood carving tools. At least one bevel is present on every cutting instrument. This is the slanting surface that extends from the edge. It's more than just a slanting surface, though. It's a cutting angle, .

As a result, the bevel allows for a particular cutting angle, which defines how the tool should be used. Bevels and how they impact cutting efficiency are well-known among experienced carvers. If you're just getting started as a woodcarver and are about to buy your first set of carving equipment, there are a few things you should know.

Some carving tools don't come with a bevel when they leave the factory. This means that you'll have to cut the angle that defines the form of the bevel yourself. Many professional woodcarvers use new tools in this manner because they prefer to control the cutting angles. They don't want to have to redo a cut.

Non-beveled edges are only recommended for woodcarvers who are familiar with sharpening knives and other cutting tools. Beveled edges function as wedges and any metal wedge functions as a knife. You can make the cutting angle (also known as the sharpening angle) just the way you like it if you know how to sharpen knives. You have complete control over the bevel.

New carving tools with pre-set bevels ground in by the manufacturer are fairly common. Nonetheless, the new carver must be mindful that it may not be the correct size or shape although the toolmaker may have produced the cutting angle.

Don't just take the bevel for granted. Determine your requirements, i.e., your basic carving activities and purchase the appropriate equipment. This isn't something you can hurry.

The carving instrument's cutting angle or the bevel's length depends on the wood strength you can carve. In simpler terms, the greater the cutting angle, the shorter and steeper the bevel. The greater the angle, the greater the edge's cutting power. The tougher the wood to be cut, the smoother the edge.

What does it all imply?

If you're trying to cut soft trees, your tool's edge should have a slight cutting angle. This is a very thin edge that produces a wide bevel (a long backward slope).

If you're trying to cut rough trees, your tool's edge should have a wide cutting angle. The result is a thicker, slanted edge with a thin bevel (short and steep).

Another crucial thing to remember is this. How much power you have when carving is determined by the cutting angle size on your edge.

More of your hands will rest on the wood if you use a carving tool with a small cutting angle and a big bevel. This allows for more control and, as a result, better carving. Your edge, sadly, isn't as good as it should be.

Less of your hands will rest on the wood if you use a carving tool with a large cutting angle and a small bevel. Since you have less control over your hands, carving could become sloppy. It's a strange phenomenon. You have a sharp edge that cuts quickly, but you're prone to making mistakes.

Since we're on the subject of bevels, here are the three most common styles used in wood carving: straight (square) bevels, rounded (convex) bevels and hollow (concave) bevels.

Straight bevels - These bevels have a straight square point, as the name suggests. For their sharpness, they have the most effective cutting and the greatest strength to the tip. Many woodcarvers prefer this style of bevelers.

Rounded Bevels - A rounded bevel has a convex profile, which is the polar opposite of a hollow bevel. Since the wedge is usually thick, it takes more time to cut it. As a result, cutting angles are large.

Hollow bevels - Hollow bevels have a concave appearance and are the polar opposite of rounded bevels. It's an unusual shape, but it's not easy to deal with. The hollowed bevel will sometimes ride up on the edge of a cut, so you'll need to keep an eye on it at all times.

You'll know a lot about any cutting tool you hold in your hand once you understand how cutting angles on beveled edges affect cutting performance. Simple errors can be prevented and you'll be on your way to becoming a professional woodcarver in no time.

CHAPTER 9

Kickbacks on Table Saws for Wood Carving

Table saws are woodworking tools that woodworkers often use. This method can be used in many ways, but it can also be a hassle if you don't know how to use it correctly. This is the most common table saw the issue, particularly when kickback occurs.

This saw is made up of a well-rounded blade connected to a shaft and powered by an electric motor. Table saws may be cheap, but their blades may be costly due to their sizes; the bigger the blades, the more they will cost. The larger blades, on the other hand, could create incredible cuts and shapes.

Kickback occurs when your saw automatically comes to a halt and your job is steered backward by

Hollow bevels - Hollow bevels have a concave appearance and are the polar opposite of rounded bevels. It's an unusual shape, but it's not easy to deal with. The hollowed bevel will sometimes ride up on the edge of a cut, so you'll need to keep an eye on it at all times.

You'll know a lot about any cutting tool you hold in your hand once you understand how cutting angles on beveled edges affect cutting performance. Simple errors can be prevented and you'll be on your way to becoming a professional woodcarver in no time.

CHAPTER 9

Kickbacks on Table Saws for Wood Carving

Table saws are woodworking tools that woodworkers often use. This method can be used in many ways, but it can also be a hassle if you don't know how to use it correctly. This is the most common table saw the issue, particularly when kickback occurs.

This saw is made up of a well-rounded blade connected to a shaft and powered by an electric motor. Table saws may be cheap, but their blades may be costly due to their sizes; the bigger the blades, the more they will cost. The larger blades, on the other hand, could create incredible cuts and shapes.

Kickback occurs when your saw automatically comes to a halt and your job is steered backward by your blade. Kickbacks could cause your blades to be redirected towards you rather than your job, which could be risky.

However, in most situations, if you follow the safety precautions outlined in your manual, these accidents will not occur and will only jeopardize your job. You might consider it the worst-case scenario, but on the bright side, if your job is destroyed, you can always start over with a new piece of wood.

Craftsmen and woodworkers are familiar with various forms of kickbacks. The most popular kickback form is straight line kickback caused by a poor saw and a low blade height.

These two factors lead to kickbacks, with the difference being that the underpowered saw slows down over time, allowing your job to be snatched and the blade height happens only when your blade is too short, causing heat to build up in your table saw's motor.

Over-the-top kickback is not a concern since the table saw's blade height is set to a low level, usually used by craftsmen who simply enjoy using the table saw. The backside is the most dangerous of all the kickbacks. It's possible the blade's pace would drive the wood back towards you.

When choosing your blades, look for one that will help you complete your mission and has a wide range of choices. Blades come in various sizes, but you should be familiar with them all because choosing or using the wrong blade could cause damage to your wood. When slicing solid objects, a ripping blade could come in handy.

Crosscut blades are excellent for forming crosscut job boundaries. If you're cutting hard and lumber core plywood, sheet goods, a veneer blade or a combination of a veneer blade and a crosscut blade, it will help you get a perfect cut.

Table saws come in handy for almost any form of woodwork. It was capable of slicing through something. It's simple to use and handle, so get one now and start making beautiful shapes and art of various sizes and having trouble using your table saw?

So, here's the best way to deal with your problem. Before you buy a tool, make sure you understand everything there is to know about it.

CHAPTER 10

Proper Proportions to Improve Your Wood Carving Caricatures

If you're reading this, you're probably interested in wood carving caricatures and wish to learn how to develop your wood carving skills. "Proportions" is the one word that will get you there.

At first glance, utilizing general proportions will make your wood carvings look pleasing and realistic. When I say "general" proportions, I mean that exact measurements to the millimeter aren't required; instead, a near approximation to correct human proportions will suffice.

Following the basic proportions of human anatomy will enhance your wood carvings' appearance and will please the eyes of those who display them. Many anatomy knowledge sources go into great detail on how long or large different body parts should be considered optimal.

After reading multiple proportional guidelines, I've decided to stick to Don Mertz's "Woodbee Carver" simple proportions codes. Mr. Mertz teaches the "Rule Of Three," which divides different body areas into thirds to make conversions for all sizes of wood carving figures simple.

Head and Face Proportions

The head is divided into thirds from top to bottom in the "Rule Of Three" analysis, with the top third being the area between the hairline and the brows. The area between the brows and the bottom of the nose is the second third and the area between the bottom of the nose and the bottom of the chin is the third.

The region under the nose can then be divided into thirds. The first third is from the nose to the lips' separation, the second third is from the lips' separation to the indention above the chin and the third is from the indention to the chin's bottom.

When viewed from the front, the lip is usually 2/3 the height of the face.

The eyes fall along the middle line from the top of the head to the bottom of the chin, dividing the head's side view into thirds. The ear starts on the centerline, laying to the back of the head and normally located in the second third of the head's side view (top of the ear at eyebrow level and bottom of the ear at the base of the nose).

Body Dimensions

Using the same "Rule Of Three" concept, the rest of the body may be separated. The body is split three times from the top of the head to the bottom of the feet.

The first third runs from the shoulder to the beltline, the second third from the beltline to the center of the knee and the third from the middle of the knee to the foot's bottom. According to drawing and wood carving conventions, the body, without the head, is roughly the length of seven heads stacked on top of each other.

Some wood carving caricatures have eight heads, so the torso (shoulders to belt line) would be three heads long and the region below the beltline would be five heads long. Experiment with the two to see which body length you prefer.

When viewed from the front or the back straight on, the shoulders are around three heads' width and are the widest portion of the body. The taller and more imposing the figure is, the broader the shoulders are.

As I previously said, precision is unimportant since few of us are truly proportionally accurate. Use these general proportions could turn your wood carving caricatures from drab to aesthetically pleasing.

CHAPTER 11

Make a Gouge Honing Board for Wood Carving

It doesn't take much to put a gouge's edge back to full sharpness after it's been properly sharpened. This is due to the edge's normal wear away from use, not because it has been hurt. When all it takes is a little honing to get it back to razor-sharpness rather than a full sharpening, there's something simple you can do.

Making a gouge honing board is one way to restore the edge to its former glory. You might use your very handy honing board to put back an edge instead of using a fine quality sharpening stone all of the time.

These are the items you'll require:

3" x 3" softwood rectangular block "2" x 1" x 2" (l x w x h)

A rouging agent is a fine abrasive paste or powder that is used for rouging.

Bench knife with a blade length of fewer than 5 inches "long-term

An old knife or a tool with a non-sharpened tip

For honing, gouges are used.

The block of wood does not have to be the right size; it just needs to be near. It could easily be made wider or longer if you want more power. You can put the honing section you'll make anywhere on the block of wood that works best for you. After all, your comfort and ease in honing gouges are what this honing board entails.

Rouging compounds come in a variety of forms. You need a material that can coat a surface quickly and easily, especially in troughs and tight corners. A rouging or polishing agent that comes in the form of a solid block is not something you like. In this case, it would be virtually useless.

Because of the tiny fixed blade, a bench knife is preferred. To make the honing surface, you don't need much of a cutting edge. All you need is something strong and sharp. Before you begin, make sure this knife has been sharpened.

Let's get started. Take the block of wood and position it where you want the honing portion to be. Start about a half-inch inwards from the width-wise side if you obey the given dimensions.

Cut a concave or positive profile into the wood with the gouge to be honed. Use the gouge's exact measurements as a reference; make sure the trough doesn't get any wider than the gouge.

The convex or negative profile will now be cut into the wood. Use the same gouge that was used to create the positive profile to create a negative profile. With a quarter of an inch, move inwards along the block of wood. That's about a quarter-inch inwards from the positive profile.

Switch the gouge over so that the trough is facing the opposite direction. Cut the negative profile of the gouge into the wood when in this location. Make sure the convex curve doesn't get any wider than the gouge.

You've just finished making a gouge honing surface. You did an outstanding job. Square the edges between the carved profiles with the bench knife. You could easily make a custom honing board with positive and negative profiles for each of your frequently used gouges.

You'll now get it ready for honing. Take the rouging compound and spread it uniformly along the trough of the positive profile with an old knife or a tool with a non-sharpened tip.

When you're done, spread the rouging compound uniformly over the negative profile's convex surface. Use the overturned gouge to pack the compound into the negative profile's tight corners gently. Your gouge honing board is now complete.

When it's time to use it, simply follow the gouge's bevel. Lay the gouge in the trough, which should match snugly with the rouging compound applied and pull it through the trough with the outside bevel flat on the honing board for the positive profile.

Turn your gouge over and fit it over the convex surface and into the close corners for the negative profile. Pull the inside bevel smoothly through the profile with the inside bevel flush with the wood. If required, add more rouging compounds. When pulling the gouges over the honing surface, use just mild pressure.

So there you have it. You have completed a gouge honing surface and know how to bring it to good use. Bear in mind that this isn't actual sharpening rather, it will restore a sharpened, undamaged edge to good working condition. It's very straightforward, but it's very successful. Consider what other kinds of fast fixes for carving tools might be devised.

Wood carving gouges must be properly cared for to preserve their durability and consistency. Carving gouges are one of the most commonly used carving instruments and as a result, they are subject to a lot of wear and tear. You can get the most out of them if you obey these guidelines.

First and foremost, invest in high-quality equipment. In the long run, quality tools will remain sharper and cost less. Do not grind your tools while sharpening them. Otherwise, you risk destroying the gouge if you don't use a whetstone and strop.

You'll also need a collection of ceramic slip stones for your carving gouges to get inside the weapon. If the sharp edges of the tools are not well-honed, the tools will not cut cleanly. When you use properly sharpened tools, you'll note a difference in your carving because they'll seem to float through the wood with little effort.

Once you've finished using your materials, clean them and make sure they're fully dry before putting them away. Plastic or leather cases may be used to store carving gouges. The most critical aspect of the case is that it holds moisture out.

You'll want to make sure the case is sturdy enough to avoid the gouges from being chipped or damaged by mistake. Place your wood carving tools in their cases in a secure location, such as a toolbox or tackle box. This will shield them from being dropped or having weighted objects fall on them by mistake.

The best tools can be ruined by poor maintenance. Through sharpening, cleaning and storing your wood carving gouges properly, you will ensure that they are easier to carve with and that your finished parts will look their best.

CHAPTER 12

How to Sharpen Straight Chisels

Sharpening carving tools is an essential part of the carving process. Sharp carving tools perform well because they cut through wood more easily, making them safer and faster to use.

It also leaves a cleaner trail in its wake. A good sharp edge necessitates less effort, which in turn necessitates less force. When less force is required, more control is possible, resulting in a safer work environment.

Sharpening carving tools can be done somehow, ranging from sandpaper to power grinders to wetstones to the strop. Use a couple of sandpaper grades and a strop is the most cost-effective process.

The amount of sharpening required is determined by how badly the blade's edge has been damaged. If the surface is scratched or dull, sand it with 400 grit sandpaper on a flat surface, such as the table's edge.

Place the blade edge down on the paper's wet surface and drag it across it at an eleven-degree angle. Use a nickel or a dime under the blade's spine is one way to get an estimated eleven-degree angle.

If your carving blade is more than three-quarters of an inch wide, lay it flat on the sharpening surface and lift the spine so you can fit the edge of nickel under it. Use a dime if it's less than three-quarters of an inch.

Drag the edge over the wet sandpaper surface until there are no more nicks and the edge is smooth. Then, using 600 grit wet sandpaper, repeat the process.

Finish by saturating the leather (strop) with white aluminum oxide until it can no longer absorb any more. To help create a paste-like consistency, add a little light oil. Be sure to wipe any sandpaper dust off your blade with a rag. You don't want any grit on your strop. Then, at the same 11-degree angle, drag the knife-edge over the strop, sharpening on both sides until you have a mirrored edge.

You can check for a sharp edge by carving across the end grain of a piece of wood carving with your knife. You should be able to see the end grain and a smooth shiny finish. You have a nick on your edge if you see a white line in your slice.

You must go back and resume the process from the beginning. Once you've achieved the edge you want on your knife, all you have to do now is strop every fifteen minutes and secure your edge while not in use.

If you're just getting started as a woodcarver, you'll soon notice how much wood chisels are used. There are many different styles and sizes. They'll need sharpening from time to time and it's nice to be able to do it yourself.

When your tools get rusty, you shouldn't have to take them to a skilled sharpener. You lose both money and time. Straight chisels are also the simplest wood carving tools to sharpen.

Sharpening straight chisels require two steps. The first step is to sharpen the tool's edge and the second is to hone it to a silky smooth finish.

Sharpening a straight chisel - This is a very basic sharpening process for straight square chisels. Begin by honing (or whetting) your knife with a coarse-grade sharpening tool. Make the shaft vertical and hit the stone with the tip.

Lower the end facing up until the surface of the edge meets the wood. Come to a complete stop right there. You've reached the right sharpening angle when the beveled face is flush with the wall.

For better power, put your index finger on the top of the beveled surface while keeping the chisel flush against the stone. Pull the stone away from the edge and towards you. Look for the burr after 10-20 repetitions. When you have reached full sharpness, a burr is a feather-like sliver of wire that will fall off the chisel's edge.

A burr will feel like sand or gravel on your edge if you run your finger over it lengthwise (never lengthwise!). If there isn't a burr, repeat the strokes before the burr is properly lifted. In case the tool has a second bevel, sharpen it in the same way you did the first. Sharpen until the burr is properly lifted.

After achieving sharpness with a coarse stone, move to a fine quality stone. This can be done with a single fine grade stone or a series of increasingly fine grade stones. Carry on sharpening in the same manner before you get a burr. If you have a second bevel, repeat the process until a burr appears. Make certain that a burr has been raised along the entire length of the chisel's edge on both sides.

Stop what you're doing and turn on the television if you're not sure. I'm not making this up. If you're going to sharpen, do it right the first time. It will have an impact on your carving ability. (What are you doing if that doesn't matter to you?)

When sharpening straight chisels, there are a few different stroke methods that are widely used. As you grip the shaft with your index finger on the top of the beveled surface, put the fingers of your other hand on top of the first. You run the tool in circles instead of dragging it towards you. If that doesn't work, try pushing the tool horizontally in one direction and then the other.

There is no one-size-fits-all solution. Experiment with different techniques to see which one works better for you. The stroke that draws away from the edge is my favorite. It's the most straightforward method for raising a burr and then detecting it.

Sharpening a skewed chisel

Straight chisels vary slightly from skewed chisels. The tip of a bent chisel is at a diagonal angle, a skewed angle and joins the side of the chisel head at a less than 90-degree acute angle.

Sharpening a bent chisel works similarly to sharpening a straight chisel. The only difference is that there is one. The bent edge must be rendered parallel to the sharpening stone's forward edge. Alternatively, the tip may be rendered perpendicular to the sharpening stone's side edge. It's good either way. If there is a second bevel, just be consistent.

Stropping with a chisel Burrs has formed all over the edge of your well-sharpened chisel. You did an excellent job. Stropping will eliminate any remaining burrs and any other micro-bits.

When it comes to stropping, you have a few options. First option: strop your edge in one direction and then the other with a free leather strap. Pull away from the edge that is parallel to the length-wise surface of the strap, with the beveled face of the chisel's edge flat on the strap.

Raise the chisel and turn it over at the end of the harness. Place the flat face of the chisel's edge on the strap on the opposite side. Pull in the opposite direction, parallel to the strap surface and away from the edge. Back and forth until the edge is silky smooth, then repeat.

A stropping board, also known as a honing board, is the second choice for stropping the chisel tip. This may be a flat rectangular surface, a paddle, a wooden bench or something you design yourself. The procedure for using a stropping board is identical to that for using a free leather harness.

A polishing compound is commonly used in conjunction with leather strops and stropping boards. It speeds up the stropping process and renders carving a breeze. It could be in the form of a liquid, paste, powder or even a solid block small enough to fit in your palm.

Stropping is a vital part of sharpening that should not be overlooked. Consider it as if you were using a chisel with a soiled tip. It certainly isn't as effective as a clean edge. Since it's dirty, you'll have to sharpen it even more often than you would normally. As a result, strop and strop well. It will improve the quality of your carving.

Beginners should be vigilant when stropping. As a beginner in this craft, the edge is often rounded rather than polished smooth. This is since the edge isn't perfectly smooth during the stropping process. With each sharpening, a secondary bevel will form, which will thicken. The only way to save the edge in the end is to remake it. That would be a huge waste of time and energy. Keep your eyes peeled.

You'll be able to sharpen any straight or skewed chisel in your toolset once you've trained those hands to do a good job. You already know a lot about sharpening carving tools. Keep up the good work. Just be alert and keep an eye out for secondary bevels.

CHAPTER 13

How To Pick The Best Style Of Wood Carving

Wood carving is a unique skill. It necessitates a great deal of patience, which a good imagination can enhance. You'll have a range of designs to choose from if you plan to become a woodcarver. A small knife and a piece of wood are everything you'll need. You might also go as far as to use power tools. So, how do you figure out which style is right for you?

Woodcarving is classified into five distinct styles. Each design differs significantly from the others. Whittling, relief carving, I chip carving intaglio carving and carving in the round are examples of these types.

Whittling is a term used in describing the process of removing. Whittling is the process of removing wood bits or shavings with a cutting blade. It's the most basic form of wood carving, but it's not wood carving art.

This is an important distinction to note since whittling is and should always be easy. All that is required is a knife and a piece of wood and, as with all other types of wood carving, whittled artifacts lack detail because they are so plain.

You can tell when holding a whittled object in your lap. Each knife stroke can be seen clearly. It is all as plain as it was hundreds of years ago, during the time of cavemen. Isn't that incredible?

Carving Chips

Chip carving requires cutting small pieces of wood (chips) from a smooth wood surface with multiple knives. Chip knives are specially crafted knives used to push or pull on the wood, cutting r downwards or upwards to free and chip.

Chip carving has risen in popularity to the point that it has become its art form. Chipping varying wood triangular shapes is the main technique. This results in complicated patterns that are mostly geometric.

To emphasize these chipped patterns, free-form lines are often used. You should let the imagination run wild.

Relief Carving

Relief Carving is the art of carving reliefs. This carving style is done on a flat back cut of wood with 3-dimensional images cut out. These are the wood carvings you see on walls, tables and countertops.

Relief carving can be divided into two categories. The visual effect produced by a low relief carving can be identified. Since there are no shadows to suggest deep carving, the result appears very shallow and is labeled as a low relief.

The inclusion of shadows in high relief carvings creates a stunning depth effect. Both styles produce carvings with a lot of depth and detail. The finished product is polished to a very smooth finish. The surface may then be painted, waxed or varnished.

Intaglio carving

Relief carving is somewhat similar to this type of wood carving but, rather than appearing to be above the wood's surface, it appears to be a part of it. Since the designs are cut deep into the wood, they are below the surface. Consider a set of old wooden rolling pins. Can you recall the cute little pictures etched into it? Intaglio carving is what it's called.

Intaglio carving is a common style among furniture makers. It's also been fitted for blank space before being carved separately and inserted into the furniture. What do you think?

It can be used in dining tables and bedroom furniture as well. It's ideal for use with wood paneling. It's often used on specialty plaques, an existing decorative piece, and the actual surface of the coffee and end tables.

Carving In The Round

This is the most advanced wood carving style. Both sides of the package can be viewed, allowing for a complete and easy view of all data. The base acts as a supporting platform or a pedestal and it is carved out of wood. It could be a human, an animal or a landscape—pretty much everything you can think of. It may be life-size or scale-modeled. When it comes to carving in the round, the sky is almost the limit.

This method of carving necessitates the use of a large range of materials. A minimum set of knives, gouges and chisels is required. The use of power tools is popular and not shocking. The end product is generally very impressive. Occasionally, a result of round carving is mistaken for a porcelain formation. The attention to detail is astounding.

Wood carving has existed since the time of the cavemen. Over time, it has developed into a beautiful piece of art. It's incredibly calming, exhilarating and satisfying. Wood carving might be the ideal hobby for you if you're looking for something different to do.

CHAPTER 14

Choosing The Proper Woodcarving Knives And Taking Care Of Them

Woodcarving knives are used to round and smooth a piece of wood so that it can be carved. The most important element of the woodcarving process is the knives. Knives of various styles are responsible for various types of curving. Any carving can be done with a well-designed knife.

Knives must be chosen with caution by a carver. The blade is one of the most important characteristics of a wood carving knife that determines its suitability for a particular task.

Depending on the task's delicacy or roughness, blades may be short or long. Aside from that, the blade must be razor-sharp. The ease of use is determined by the high degree of sharpness. A specialist usually sharpens the blade.

Choosing a wood carving knife can be extremely important to the carving project's success. This must be done with great caution. When choosing a wood carving knife, the blade and handle are the most important features to consider. The blade should be short if the task needs delicate handling and longer if it requires rough handling.

The handle must be a good match for the carver's hand. If the handle doesn't fit correctly, the carver will have to work extra hard to achieve the necessary detail level.

In that case, he may become fatigued more easily than normal and the quality of his work may suffer as a result. Each wood carving knife is made uniquely. As a result, the carver must choose the ideally suited to his hand and intended use.

The sharpness of the blade is also essential in making the carver's job easier. For two reasons, the sharp or dull edge is crucial. First, the blunt edge degrades the work's consistency by obstructing the delivery of fine information. Second, the blunt edge adds to the force applied to the knife, which can be harmful if the blade slips and injures the carver's side.

There are two ways to ensure that the blades have a sharp edge. You need to keep them from being easily blunted. Surprisingly, this can be accomplished easily by correctly arranging the blades.

The bang among the wood carving power tools will damage the blades if they are stored in a box or compartment in an unorganized manner. Consequently, the knives should be hanging by their handles or kept separate in a cabinet with compartments.

Second, they must be sharpened once they have become blunt. A specialist can preferably perform sharpening, but for beginner carvers, this is a must. Sharpening knives may be done with stone sharpeners, power grinders or leather strops by professional carvers. The stones may be hard or soft and they require either oil or water. Knives can be sharpened by repeatedly scraping them against the stones.

Sharpening knives with motorized power grinders are easy, but wood carving power tools must be kept against the wheel while the wheel is spinning away from the knife. The leather strops' micro-abrasive surface can also be used to sharpen knives.

The climate in which the knives are stored is also a significant factor. Heat and cold should be kept at a moderate level and moisture should be kept to a minimum. The right wood carving power tools and the right degree of care for these knives, will make the job of a carver much easier. Some of the best woodcarving works could be created as a result of his creativity.

Another significant aspect is how the knives are carried. The right form and length of the handle ensure this. A carver may become extremely tired very quickly if the handle is misaligned. The handle's ergonomic style is appealing. Since each wood carving tool's knife is slightly different, the carver must choose the better for his hand.

The carver's preference and the mission he intends to achieve with the knives direct the purchasing decision. However, after purchasing the knives, a carver must complete those tasks. These responsibilities include both the proper care of the knives and their safe use.

The wood carving materials, for starters, are well apart from one another. Putting them together in a random order could result in one of them slamming into another. The edges can become blunt as a result of the friction. The carving task is highly painful and unreliable due to the blunt edges.

Furthermore, the blunt edge can force the carver to use excessively high carving pressure. This is risky if the knife falls and injures the carver. As a result, a woodcarving knife with a blunt or dull point is undesirable. Wood carving tools may be hung separately or kept arranged in their compartments.

Another method is to sharpen the edges regularly. The sharp edge can carve woods quickly and accurately. The wood carving knife should be sharpened by a specialist for the novice or beginner-level carvers. Sharpening knives with proper wood carving power tools are required for an accomplished carver.

Sharpening a carving knife requires a few wood carving power tools. One of these wood carving power tools is a sharpening hammer. Sharpening stones are classified into two categories: harder and softer. The stones need oil and water.

The blade must be drawn over the stone repeatedly until it is acutely sharp. Power grinders have rotating motorized wheels. Sharpening the blades requires holding them against the wheel.

When using a power grinder, you should wear safety glasses. Finally, you can use leather to sharpen blades. Sharpening a blade is a breeze with the leather's incredibly fine abrasive surface.

The blades must be kept in a secure place. Heat and cold should not be applied to the wood carving knife. The moisture level should not be too high or too low.

The proper care of woodcarving knives is necessary for a good carving project. A skilled carver understands that caring for the wood carving knife is just as important as performing the job itself. Beginner carvers should be aware of this and begin learning how to care for their tools. Choosing the right wood carving tools and caring for them properly can result in high-quality carving work.

CHAPTER 15

Protecting Your Wood Carving Knife Edges

It's something we've always done. We sliced the Donut box lid open with a carving knife, and then got up to answer the phone with a chisel placed on our knee, only for it to fall to the floor and ruin the tip. (To make it worse, it was just a telemarketer!)

Things like this happen to all of us and we wonder why our tools aren't sharpening themselves. Our tools' life span would be significantly extended if we can learn to prevent these incidents from happening.

Things that can wreak havoc on your edges

Sandpaper is a type of sandpaper that is on any edge, and sandpaper is possibly the worst. It's made up of the same Aluminum Oxide or Silicon Carbide particles that go into making your knife's edge in the first place. Carve as close to done as you can without using sandpaper while carving a piece that will inevitably need to be sanded.

You can't go back to carving after you've begun sanding your carving. When you sand, you leave abrasive sandpaper particles in and on your carving, which can rub against the edge when you use your knife to brush up an area that has been sanded, dulling it.

Other resources

Most of these tools have undergone a lengthy heat treatment procedure to harden them. They would become boring if they bang against each other. Misuse of the equipment is a major no-no.

This is something I've done before. I've reached the point where I can begin sanding my carving, so I used my carving knife to break the sandpaper into smaller bits. It's not a good idea. To do this, you'll need a cheap knife.

The bench or table

Tools fall off the table or are forced onto the floor. To prevent your knives from slipping, put them on a tray with a rubber drawer liner glued to the bottom. My lining was $2.50 for a 6-foot roll at Home Depot.

Please don't.

Knives and chisels should be held in the same compartment. Each tool should be held in its compartment. When you keep these tools in the same compartment, the hard steel of the tools bangs against each other as you walk to your car after a carving club meeting, dulling them.

Sandpaper should not be stored with your knives; instead, it should be kept in a separate jar. These particles rub your tools when they fall into your bag or package.

Carry out.

Keep a scavenging knife in your pocket. Slice up your sandpaper, cut open the super glue and scrape the paint off your fingernails with this knife.

Place the tools back on the table or in positions where they won't roll off or into each other.

Keep your equipment in a sheath. You'll be able to keep all of your tools intact if you do it this way.

I've seen a lot of options for sheaths.

Wine corks may be used as chisels and blades.

Carving your sheaths in the form of thumbs, ducks and other animals have been used in Woodcarving Illustrated.

Simply cut a block of styrofoam that is longer than your blade and mount it.

Foam Core - Request foam-core cutoffs from your nearest picture frame. It's a styrene sheet with both sides coated in the paper. It's also available in various colors. After that, you can cut it to size with your tools.

Wrap a piece of leather around your blade and glue it in place.

Phone books - At a show, I saw a woman roll up a phonebook and tape it together to place her knife blades between the covers. We've all taken the time to learn how to sharpen our tools to a razor's edge; now it's time to defend them!

CHAPTER 16

Wood Carving Skill Make Money From Wood Carvings, Without You Carving Anything

Wood carving is a technical art. Patience, focus and time are needed. There are many lovely wood sculptures for sale at the store, but do you know how a craftsman works with wood? There are three types of wood carving abilities.

1. Hand carving. This wood carving expertise necessitates more time and focus. Usually, a carver may begin a new carving by selecting a good wood, determined by the wood's estimated size and outer shape the carver wishes to carve. If the carving is to be big, many pieces may be fixed together.

After the general shape has been developed, the carver can add information with various carving tools. (gouge, carving knife Chisel, V-tool and veneer are some of the tools) After the carving is completed, the carver may use natural oils to seal or stain the wood, such as linseed oil or walnut, to protect it from dirt and moisture.

2. Make a paper model

In this area, this is the most commonly used skill. Some woodwork suppliers do not have professional carvers on board. As a result, they sometimes sketch out the shape of the characters they want to carve on the wood on paper, and then paste the paper on the wood for the carvers to follow the paper's lines. The paper model wood carving saves a lot of time, but the finished wood carving isn't as accurate as it could be.

3. The computer.

Nowadays, machine carving is also commonly used. Since machines can only operate on flat surfaces, it is difficult to carve three-dimensional work with them. We can easily answer the question "why are handmade carvings so much more costly than others?" by comparing the sculpture skills mentioned above.

Carvings in wood have always been common. Most people who have traveled to places like Indonesia or the Philippines have seen them is handcrafted. The professional carvers sit cross-legged on the floor, chipping away at a piece of wood until they have carved an elephant, a person's head or some other wonderful carving.

These one-of-a-kind things often tend to be much more special than anything we might produce. One day you go to a local art store and see a shelf full of similar wood carvings. How do they make them all look alike?

Isn't it true that one craftsman can't be that precise every time?

No, they won't be able to. A wood-carving machine is a key to this mass-production. This is where you can launch your own lucrative woodcarving business without ever having to raise a single carving stone.

The wood carving machines take a single carving and duplicate it. It's almost magical how they function. The computer traces the original carving and carves a second copy as it goes. The two-hundred-dollar carving becomes a two-hundred-dollar carving. The possibilities are limitless.

Since each one is similar to the first, they can all be sold for the same price. Stool seats, the bookends, Christmas tree decorations and everything else you can find can all be replicated in the same level of detail as the original.

The machine and the wood are the only expenses you'll have to make. Any of these wood carving devices can be found for as little as a couple of hundred dollars on eBay.

If you made a copy of a carving sold for $200 the first time, you might sell the second one for the same price and recoup the wood carving machine's cost with only one carving! You can also use any kind of wood that you can find and free wood can be found.

Many people have trees in their gardens that they no longer want and have them removed. The trunk is sometimes chopped up for firewood. However, if you contact anyone you know who has recently had a tree cut down; you might be able to retrieve some of the wood before it is broken up into smaller pieces.

They'll be relieved to get it off their back and they're unlikely to call for any compensation. It's worth contacting your local tree surgeons or other companies that cut down trees to see if they can get the wood for you for a reasonable price.You'll be making wood carvings before you know it.

CHAPTER 17

Woodcarving Tips to Help You Along

Wood carving is a satisfying and enjoyable activity for both skilled and beginner artists. Nothing compares to the satisfaction of transforming a material scrap into something useful that you can show in your home, offer a gift or sell for profit. Also, to the necessary skills, the right supplies for wood carving are needed.

Woodworking is a wonderful hobby that can create beautiful crafts and furniture passed down through the generations. Woodworking is becoming a successful hobby and a lucrative business.

A professional woodworker with access to a well-equipped workshop may build simple birdhouses and more complex furniture. Woods for raw materials are available at lumber retail stores and hobby supply stores.

Some people are perplexed as to what a board foot is. A board foot is a measurement unit used in the wood industry. It measures 1 foot long, 1 foot wide and 1 inch thick. It is important to remember that the thickness is nominal. A 1-inch board is usually 13/16 thick after drying and surfacing. Ten board feet are equivalent to a board that is 10 feet long, 1 foot high and 1 inch thick.

I'm frequently asked, "What's the best way to deal with the glue squeeze-out problem?"

The answer is clear. Make sure you use the right amount of glue!

A glue-starved joint is the (obvious) threat. Wipe away any leftover glue with a wet sponge or paper towel as soon as possible. According to some woodworkers, the water-glue mixture can soak into the wood and show up until the piece is completed. Many others, including myself, believe that this is not a problem.

Allowing the adhesive to harden a little before chiseling or scraping it off is another choice. The efficacy of this process is likely to be determined by the type of wood and finish used. If you've been woodworking for a long time or are considering it as a hobby, bear in mind that it necessitates the use of tools and techniques that are potentially dangerous.

As a result, workshop safety is a top priority for any woodworker. When working in the shop, remember to protect your eyes, ears and lungs and exercise extreme caution when using hand and power tools.

If you've been woodworking for a long time or are considering it as a hobby, keep in mind that it necessitates the use of tools and techniques that are potentially dangerous.

As a result, workshop safety is a top priority for any woodworker. It is important to protect your eyes, ears and lungs when operating in the shop and exercise extreme caution while using hand and power tools.

The possibilities for making a sculpture or figurine out of a piece of wood are infinite. It's a good idea to have a roadmap for what you want to make before choosing the right equipment. Making sketches or even taking pictures of the image you want to carve creates a mental image that will help you stay on track until the carving starts.

Before you start shopping for materials, familiarize yourself with the various wood carving forms, such as relief carving, chip carving and whittling. Finally, before selecting carving materials, you must first determine the type of wood to use.

The carving knife is the most basic tool for wood carving. These knives are available in shapes, sizes, and blade angles and are used for various tasks, including cutting, paring, and smoothing wood.

Many of the blades are designed for long-term use in wood carving and the handles are designed for ease of use. Always do your homework to find the right knife for the job at hand.

The gouge is another valuable method. This is a wood carving instrument with a curved cutting edge used to carve hollows, rounds and sweeping curves. Gouges come in a range of shapes, sizes and angles, much like normal carving knives.

When choosing the right variety of tools, such as gouges, pay careful attention to relative proportions, which refers to the size of a cut or groove compared to the size of other cuts and the piece's overall size.

The chisel, for example, has a straight cutting edge that can be used to cut lines and clean up flat surfaces. Chisels may also be used for wedging and are commonly used in combination with hammers to drive into the wood.

Once again, selecting the appropriate type is critical. There are many different types of chisels to choose from, including ass, carving, corner and framing chisels. Remember to analyze and review the plans before settling on a particular method.

As your project progresses, you can discover that your current resources are inadequate for a specific task. More specialized equipment, such as a V-tool, a veneer or a router, may be needed in the future.

Know that there is a tool for any form of cut you can think of; just do some homework and you'll find what you're looking for. A mallet and a special screw for holding your project to a table can also be useful additions to your wood carving tools.

CONCLUSION

Learning the fundamentals of carving takes some time while mastering the technique takes a lifetime. The path from beginner to master, however long it takes, can be a lot of fun and result in a lot of good and satisfying bits.

Fortunately, with a few deft chisel motions, you will master the fundamentals of all carving. Carving strokes obey a few rules: carve with the grain, work against the waste rather than the shape and carve from the shortest to the longest grain length.

The moves are straightforward, but nothing beats practice. With enough practice, you'll be able to tell whether you're following these basic rules by the feel and even the sound of a chisel slicing through the wood.

Choosing the best wood species for a project is just as critical in carving as it is in any other form of woodworking, if not more so because you can't rely on a tool to do the work for you. Begin with softwoods with fine grain, such as basswood. Then, as your ability improves, you can carve more difficult, strongly figured hardwoods.

A carver's workshop can evolve. In any case, compared to a woodworking store, which typically has three or more big machines and a stable of power tools and hand tools, it's very easy.

In a room big enough for a workbench and a tool chest, you can get by very nicely. You can add another work surface and a band saw if you have a little more space, which is useful for reducing blanks to rough size before carving.

Firm clamping is important for protection, but it presents specific challenges due to the irregular shapes that a carver often encounters. A shifting workpiece may cause the carver to lose control of the chisel, resulting in damage to the carver's piece or injury.

When working with a sharp tool, hold both hands behind the blade at all times. To prevent nasty cuts when you reach for a stone, spread your chisels with the edges facing away from you. Do remember to wear comfortable footwear. Unprotected feet may be severely injured by a gouge or other tool that falls from a workbench.

Since carving should be done standing up, choose a workshop floor with carpeting or an anti-fatigue pad. Particularly if you work for many hours at a time, your feet, legs and back will notice the difference. If you drop one of your tools, the padded surface will cover the edges.

As the old-timers call it, there's woodcarving and whittling, with the latter being the more ancient of the two. To begin carving, you'll need three things: 1. a whittling knife or a six-piece simple carving kit, 2. a softwood and 3. your imagination and desire.

You can advance to chainsaws and hardwoods as your skills grow, but for now, we'll stick with the basics. The following tools are included in the simple six-piece carving set: A straight gouger, a straight veneer, a straight chisel, a bent v-tool, a straight skew and a bent chisel are among the tools available.

These tools come with some handle shapes, so you can pick which one feels more secure in your hand. The majority of sets are under $50.00. There are four basic styles of woodcarving, each of which may necessitate the use of different tools.

As previously mentioned, whittling is the oldest of these and only includes a carving knife. There's also Round Carving, Relief Carving and Chip Carving.

Basswood, Fir and Cottonwood are the perfect woods for hand carvers. You will not produce the desired results if you use either too soft or too rough wood. The rest is up to you once you have the right tools and wood.

Woodcarving is an extremely inexpensive hobby that helps the artist to avoid the burdens we all face by letting the day's issues float to the floor with the shavings.

Why don't you try creating a simple design now, using those mentioned above useful and interesting woodcarving details?

Thanks for Reading

Lightning Source UK Ltd.
Milton Keynes UK
UKHW021245270521
384475UK00008B/1553

Lightning Source UK Ltd.
Milton Keynes UK
UKOW050007090313

207392UK00009B/166/P